BIBLE PROPHECY
MADE CLEAR

BIBLE PROPHECY MADE CLEAR

A User-Friendly Look at the End Times

Previously published as *Bible Prophecy for Blockheads*

DOUGLAS CONNELLY

ZONDERVAN

Bible Prophecy Made Clear
Copyright © 2002 by Douglas Connelly

Previously published as *Bible Prophecy for Blockheads.*

This book is also available as a Zondervan ebook.

Requests for information should be addressed to:
Zondervan, 3900 *Sparks Drive SE, Grand Rapids, Michigan,* 49546

This edition ISBN: 978-0-310-59711-7

The Library of Congress Cataloged the original edition as follows:

Connelly, Douglas, 1949-
    The Bible for blockheads : a user-friendly look at the Good Book / Douglas Connelly. — Rev. ed.
      p. cm.
    Includes bibliographical references.
    ISBN-13: 978-0-310-27388-2
    ISBN-10: 0-310-27388-9
    1. Bible—Introductions. I. Title.
BS475.2.C67 2007
220.6'1—dc22   2007006709

Cover design: Haley Culver
Cover image: Shutterstock
Interior design: Sherri L. Hoffman
Interior illustrations: Patten Illustration

Printed in the United States of America

17 18 19 20 21 22 23 24 25 26 27 /DHV/ 20 19 18 17 16 15 14 13 12 11 10 9 8 7 6 5 4 3 2 1

Contents

Chapter 1 The End Is Near (or Something Like That) — 7

Chapter 2 "I Will Return": Jesus' Second Coming — 27

Chapter 3 Terror at Every Turn: The Tribulation — 43

Chapter 4 Enter the Beast: The Antichrist — 71

Chapter 5 The Great Disappearance: The Rapture — 95

Chapter 6 The Last World War: The Battle of Armageddon — 115

Chapter 7 Thy Kingdom Come: The Millennium — 131

Chapter 8 Your Personal Future: Death and What Comes After — 161

Chapter 9 Judgment Day: Everyone's Future Accountability to God — 175

Chapter 10 The Never-Ending Story: Heaven — 193

Chapter 11 A Survival Guide for the Future — 207

A Word of Thanks — 217

CHAPTER 1

The End Is Near
(or Something Like That)

The End Is Near
(or Something Like That)

—— **Heads Up** ——————————————————

 ▸ God knows the future — but has he told us?
 ▸ Reading the Bible for fun and prophet
 ▸ How to spot a prophecy fake

We all want to know the future. Think about your own life — your job, your marriage, your friends, your grades, your kids, your investments. We could have fabulous success and avoid most of life's problems if we could just get a glimpse of what the future holds.

The calendar change to a new millennium, the terrorist attacks of September 11, 2001, the continual shifting of political alliances in our world, the unpredictability of the economy — all these facts have sparked a renewed interest in the future, and particularly in the future according to the Bible.

Consider this:

- 67 percent of Americans (including one-third of those who say they never attend church) believe that Jesus Christ will return to earth someday.
- 49 percent believe that there will be an Antichrist.
- 44 percent believe that God will bring about the end of human history — and 20 percent think it will be within the next few decades.

We are very interested in what the Bible says about the future, but the problem is that prophecy seems to be such a confusing mix of different views, strange charts, mysterious visions, and weird symbols. It's too far-out for most people!

This book is written to help you sort things out with respect to God's plan for the future. We'll start with the basics and keep it simple and clear every step of the way. You may feel like a blockhead when it comes to prophecy, but you won't be a blockhead for long.

Prophecy is what God says about the future. He is the only person who knows with absolute certainty what will happen — and he knows it all. God hasn't told us *everything* about the future, but he has told us a lot. The good part is we can trust what he says. Here's God's own testimony about his ability to predict the future:

> I am God, and there is no other;
> I am God, and there is none like me.
> I make known the end from the beginning,
>   from ancient times, what is still to come.
> I say: My purpose will stand,
>   and I will do all that I please. (Isaiah 46:9 – 10)

In four words, **God knows the future.**

This book will explore what God has told us about future events. Some of what he says is scary; some is fabulous. Some elements in the future are clearly explained; some we have to piece together from a few hints. But it's *all* fascinating stuff!

Three kinds of readers will find this book helpful:

Reader #1: A Newbie

If you've never studied prophecy and get confused sometimes by all the jargon Christians throw around, this book will help you figure it all out. I've written with prophecy newbies in mind.

Reader #2: You've Been Around Awhile

Maybe you feel like you know a lot about prophecy, but you've only been exposed to one view about how future events will unfold. If you

---

Eschatology

The big theological word for the study of what the Bible teaches about the future is *eschatology* (ess-ka-**tol**-ogy). It means "the study of last things." Most of the biblical information about the future centers around the wrap-up of human history and eternity — the last things on humanity's timeline.

are saying, "You mean there's more than one view?" then this book is for you, too. I have tried to take a fair and honest look at all the major approaches to biblical prophecy. I have my own particular position, of course, but I've tried to give everyone a voice. You may find yourself changing some aspects of what you believe — or you may find your view strengthened by what you read about other positions. I don't try to cram one view down everyone's throat. I want this book to be a guide to help you make your own decisions based on all the relevant evidence.

Reader #3: You're Just Not Sure

You may not believe any of this prophecy stuff and you just picked up this book out of curiosity or even contempt. That's okay, too! I hope you'll approach what's here with an open mind. You may find your life changed by what you read.

My goal is to make the journey profitable and fun. I've taken a light-hearted approach but not a light-headed one. You will enjoy the journey, but it will also enrich your mind and maybe even transform your life.

God Has Spoken

God has given us information about the future in a unique book — the Bible. The word *Bible* means "the books." The Bible is one book, but it is also a collection of sixty-six individual books written over a period of sixteen hundred years by at least forty different authors.

The Bible is divided into two main sections — the Old Testament (or Hebrew Bible) and the New Testament. The Old Testament focuses on God's interaction with the people of Israel. The New Testament, written later, focuses on Jesus and his early followers (called Christians). The Bible is the story of God seeking and rescuing people who were far from him.

The books of the Bible were collected over the years and arranged in the order we have in our present Bible. When the Bible began to be printed in book form around A.D. 1550, chapters and verses were added to make it easier to find a specific text. Today we have a standard way of writing references to Bible verses. *Revelation 3:20*, for example, means the book of *Revelation* (the biblical book), *chapter 3* (the chapter number is listed to the left of the colon), *verse 20* (the verse number is listed to the right of the colon). The Bible reference is the "address" of the verse in the Bible. You can pick up any Bible and find the book of Revelation (the last book in the New Testament). In the third chapter, verse 20, you will read these words spoken to the apostle John by Jesus:

> Here I am! I stand at the door and knock. If anyone hears my voice and opens the door, I will come in and eat with him, and he with me.

Not every version of the Bible has those exact words, but the sense will be the same.

Down through the centuries the Bible has been translated into other languages from the ancient languages in which it was written. A translation of the Bible is called a *version* of the Bible. In this book I almost always quote from the *New International Version* (abbreviated NIV), the most widely used English-language version today. Other versions you may see or may own are the Authorized or King James Version (AV, KJV), the *New American Standard Bible* (NASB), or the *New Revised Standard Version* (NRSV). Catholic readers may have the *New American Bible* (NAB) or the *Jerusalem Bible* (JB).

All versions or translation of the Bible attempt to express accurately in a new language the meaning of the original writings. The best version for you is the one you will actually read!

Christians look at the Bible as more than just a collection of dusty religious writings. The Bible is God's word to us — God's truth written in human language. The Bible itself claims to originate with God, not with those humans who wrote it. This is not just human beings reflecting on who God is and how God acts; this is God revealing to human beings exactly who he is and what he has done.

That's important to remember as you read what the Bible says about the future. These are not the predictions of people naively hoping for a happy, pie-in-the-sky ending or of doomsdayers trying to scare people with stories of catastrophes. This is God telling us what he knows will happen and what he has planned to happen. God spoke the truth to the Bible's original writers, and he still speaks to us today through their writings.

You may not agree that the Bible is God's book. You may think that the Bible's statements about the future were simply the whacked-out ideas of some ancient hippies who were spaced out on first-century marijuana. (That idea has actually been proposed.) It's okay to be skeptical, but I hope you will pursue your interest in prophecy anyway. What you will discover as you read is that the Bible can defend itself. You may find God speaking to *you* when you least expect it!

The Key Players

Almost every book in the Bible has prophecy in it — some kind of prediction about the future or about an end-time event. A few biblical books, however, are almost completely about future events — future to the writer and future to us. You will have a jump start on your understanding if you have some background on these first-string players.

Daniel

Daniel is the Old Testament point man when it comes to prophecy. You may know him as the man who survived the lions' den, but he has a lot more on his résumé than that. Daniel spent most of his life in the city of Babylon, far from his homeland in Israel. He worked for a succession of pagan Babylonian kings. Sometimes Daniel held positions of honor, and sometimes he was forgotten — until a crisis arose that required the expertise of a person in touch with God.

Over the years, through visions, dreams, and direct communication, God gave Daniel an incredible amount of information about Israel's future. Some of what God told Daniel came about in the four hundred years that followed Daniel's death. Daniel accurately predicted the rise of the Persian Empire, the conquests of Alexander the Great, the division of Alexander's kingdom, and the persecution Israel would suffer under an evil Syrian king. Daniel's predictions were so accurate that critics of the Bible say that Daniel had to have lived *after* all these events happened. He must have only pretended to write an ancient document. No one (the critics say) could have predicted Israel's history so precisely hundreds of years earlier. Well, no one but *God,* that is! And that's exactly what Christians claim. Daniel wrote accurately about the future because he wrote under God's direction. I'm sure Daniel didn't even understand some of the stuff he wrote, but he put it down at God's command.

Two-thirds of Daniel's predictions have already been fulfilled — it's ancient history — but that final third is of vital interest to us. Our logic in this is easy to follow: If part of Daniel's prophecies happened precisely as he predicted, we can safely assume that the rest of Daniel's prophecies will take place in the future *just as precisely.* If his predictions about an evil Syrian king came true, it's not hard to believe that his predictions about a still-future evil king will also come true.

What puts the final stamp of approval on Daniel's book for me is that Jesus believed Daniel really existed (he referred to "the prophet Daniel" in Matthew 24:15). Jesus even quoted Daniel's writings as an accurate portrayal of events related to Jesus' future return to earth in glory (Mark 14:62 quotes Daniel 7:13).

Daniel will have a lot to say to us about how God's future plan will unfold.

Ezekiel

Another key Old Testament player on the prophecy team is Ezekiel. Zeke was a powerful preacher, a creative communicator, and at times was a little weird! He lived in Babylon, like Daniel did, but he didn't minister in the king's palace. Ezekiel's audience were the thousands of Jews who had been deported to Babylon from the homeland of Israel. They were a sad, despondent group, but Ezekiel tried to keep their eyes focused on the awesome majesty of God.

Ezekiel tells us how God will restore his people Israel in the future. What seems spiritually to be a valley of dry bones, dead and unresponsive to God and beyond hope, will miraculously emerge as a new people, filled and energized by God's Spirit. (That sentence is based on Ezekiel's most famous vision — the valley of dry bones — recorded in Ezekiel 37.) Ezekiel also pictures the Messiah's future Kingdom and the glorious Temple that will be the place of our worship during that Kingdom (Ezekiel 40 – 48).

Zechariah

The prophet Zechariah focused on the Messiah's Kingdom, too. But instead of emphasizing the glory of the Kingdom, Zechariah emphasized the glory of the King.

Zechariah lived in Jerusalem after the captives in Babylon returned to their homeland. They returned to a destroyed city and a desolate country. Zechariah's job was to remind the people that God had not forgotten his promises. The Messiah would still come; the Messiah would yet rule over the world. God had *not* forgotten.

Other Old Testament Voices

Other Old Testament books that speak at some length about future events are Isaiah, Joel, and Zephaniah. Even some of the psalms are prophetic and tell us about the Messiah's ultimate victory over evil and the majesty of the coming Kingdom.

The Gospels

The first four books of the New Testament tell the story of Jesus — from four different perspectives. Jesus talked a lot about the future for both the nation of Israel and his new movement called the church. Many of Jesus' parables focused on future events. The Gospels also record some of the Bible's clearest promises about Jesus' return. One scholar has counted 238 verses from the Gospels that speak to Jesus' second coming — more than half of the verses in the entire New Testament on the subject.

Matthew, the author of the first Gospel in our arrangement of the New Testament, records more of Jesus' predictions than any of the other Gospel writers. Matthew was one of Jesus' closest followers during his ministry, so he was writing down the things he had heard directly from Jesus. Matthew wrote to present Jesus as the King, and we learn in his Gospel how we are to live as loyal subjects of King Jesus. We also learn about the Kingdom in this Gospel — the Kingdom today and the Kingdom in the future.

One of the longest sermons Jesus gave about the future is recorded in Matthew 24 and 25. It's called the Olivet discourse (because Jesus spoke the words on the Mount of Olives, looking down over the city of Jerusalem). That's also when Jesus made his important statement that "no one knows" the day when Jesus will return — no one except God the Father. (Check it out in Matthew 24:36.)

First and Second Thessalonians

These two letters written by Paul, one of the most significant leaders of the early Christian movement, fill in some details about the future that are only hinted at in other books. Paul makes prophetic statements in some of his other letters, but most of what we learn from Paul about God's future plan is drawn from these two letters.

Revelation

The premier book of the Bible on future events is the book of Revelation. It was written by the apostle John (another one of Jesus' closest followers) when he was exiled on the prison island of Patmos. Domitian, the Roman emperor, was trying to wipe out the Christian community, and so he sent John, the last living apostle, into exile. Too bad for Domitian that God had other plans! God gave John (and the rest of us) a powerful story of the triumph of Jesus over all evil forever.

John received the message of Revelation in a series of visions. Some are visions of heaven; some are visions of earth. They are filled with symbols and images and beasts and angels. For example, in Revelation 5:6, John looked into heaven and saw a lamb standing in front of the throne of God. We are told right in the passage that the lamb is Jesus. Obviously Jesus is not a literal lamb with four legs and wool! The lamb is a symbol; it communicates certain aspects of Jesus' character and

APOCALYPSE NOW!

The word *Apocalypse* (a-**pok**-a-lips) is the English spelling of the first Greek word in the original text of the book of Revelation. It means "revealing" or "unveiling." Writers in the ancient world would often title a book by the first important word in the text. You will sometimes hear the book of Revelation referred to as "the Apocalypse." In our popular culture, the word has come to mean a catastrophe or an end-of-the-world event.

Amos 3:7

Surely the Sovereign LORD does nothing without revealing his plan to his servants the prophets.

ministry. He was the supreme sacrifice for sin. All throughout the Old Testament the sacrificial lambs had pictured Jesus' final sacrifice on the cross. In other passages of Scripture Jesus is called "the Lamb of God." So we can figure out the symbols by looking carefully at any interpretation John gives us and by comparing the symbols with other passages of Scripture.

Later in Revelation John sees a beast rise out of the sea (the vision is in chapter 13). The beast has the features of a leopard, a bear, and a lion. Furthermore the beast has seven heads and ten horns! John doesn't clearly identify who or what this beast represents — and Christians have come up with all kinds of suggestions! By looking at what the beast does and by comparing this passage in Revelation with other passages of Scripture, we can conclude that this beast represents a powerful person (or institution) that sets itself against God and seeks to destroy God's people.

Remember as you read Revelation that John saw these visions literally come to life before his eyes. He didn't just read what would happen — he saw it! A few times John had a difficult time even coming up with the words to describe what he was seeing. But it is the dramatic visualization that makes such a powerful impact on those of us who read it almost two thousand years later.

We will read a lot from the books of Revelation and Daniel and Matthew in this book. Don't be intimidated or nervous about biblical prophecy. Even the "experts" struggle with some of this stuff. Nobody has all the answers (not even me)! The good news is that you can understand most of what Revelation says — or Daniel or Paul or Jesus — and in the process you will learn about what God has in store for *your* future.

HELP FILE
TELLING THE TRUTH

God's prophets come on the scene all throughout the Old and New Testaments. But God's people also had to contend with *false prophets* — men and women who claimed to speak for God but didn't. Some of the false prophets could have been deceived or mentally unstable — like the man who stands in our city on the downtown mall and announces to everyone who passes by that he is Jesus Christ. Some were deluded, but most false prophets were deceivers. They were in the prophet business for profit! They liked being interviewed on *Good Morning, World* or having their faces on the cover of the supermarket tabloids. So they claimed to have a word from God, but it was a lie.

We still have false prophets who claim to speak for God. Some of them are inside the Christian community, trying to make a name for themselves or trying to cash in on gullible Christians. Other false prophets use magic or psychic powers to foretell the future — and some of them are pretty good. They do tap into a source of supernatural power, but it's not God. These people have come under the influence of demons — sinful angels controlled by Satan.

God gave his people a series of tests for ferreting out false prophets. These six tests are a good place to start when someone comes along who claims to know the future or who makes demands in God's name.

Test #1: The True Prophet Is to Speak in the Name of the Lord, the True God

According to the Old Testament, if a prophet spoke in the name of Baal (pronounced **bay**-uhl; a false god worshiped by Israel's enemies), that prophet was to be put to death. (Read it yourself in Deuteronomy 13:1 – 5 and 18:20.) Today if someone speaks a message from someone other than the true God, we don't put him to death — we just walk away. A few Christians think it's cool to get everyone's opinion on how the future will unfold, throw the Bible's perspective in the mix for good measure, and then say, "I'm open to lots of different views." To do so is to play a dangerous game! We can certainly study what others believe, but the measure of truth is what God has clearly said in the Bible.

Test #2: The True Prophet Speaks Only at the Lord's Command

False prophets usually have tricks or slick techniques to get God's attention. Witchcraft, sorcery, astrology, magic spells, and reading omens are all ways human beings try to manipulate God. True prophets speak only after they first receive a message from God (Deuteronomy 18:10 – 12; Ezekiel 12:24; Micah 3:7).

Test #3: A Genuine Prophet Backs Up His Message with a Holy, God-Honoring Life

If a drunkard or an immoral man or woman claims to speak for God, their lifestyle invalidates their message. Arrogance, sexual immorality, and greed are the marks of a false prophet. (Check out 2 Peter 2:10 – 12 and Jude 4–19; you can also read Isaiah 28:7; Hosea 9:7 – 9; and Micah 3:11.) An early church writer said, "The only person who is a prophet is the one who walks in the ways of the Lord" (this is from the *Didache*, a tract written in the second century A.D.). Jesus said that true and false prophets would be known by their fruit — by their words and actions (Matthew 7:15 – 20).

Test #4: The True Prophet (Sometimes) Authenticates His Message with a Miracle

God demonstrated to the people of Israel that Moses was his true messenger when Moses' wooden staff was cast to the ground and it became a snake (Exodus 4:1 – 5). But an astonishing miracle by itself is never enough to prove that a prophet speaks from God (Deuteronomy 13:1 – 3). The true test of a prophet is the content of his message, not his miracle.

Test #5: The True Prophet's Message Is Always in Harmony with What God Has Already Said

Any prophet who denies that Jesus is God the Son, for example, is a false prophet. Walk away. Don't buy his book or cassette tape series or attend his meetings (1 John 4:1 – 3). Anyone leading Christians away from the true message about Jesus is to be rejected — even if the messenger is an angel! (Read Paul's curse in Galatians 1:8 – 9.)

Test #6: The True Prophet's Message Always Comes True

No "two out of three" or "pretty close" in this game. God's prophet has it right every time (Deuteronomy 18:21 – 22).

All the elements have to be in place. If a prophet fails the test at any point, his message is rejected.

Jeremiah, an Old Testament prophet, heard a self-proclaimed prophet named Hananiah predict that God was going to set the people of Israel free from the oppressive rule of Babylon in *two* years. Jeremiah knew that wasn't true. God had already revealed through Jeremiah that the people would languish under the Babylonian boot for *seventy* years. (Warning! Warning! Hananiah just failed test #5!) Jeremiah said, in effect, "Hananiah, the Lord has not sent you, for you are speaking lies — and to prove that I am a true prophet, I predict that you will die this year!" The last verse of the chapter says: "In the seventh month of that same year, Hananiah the prophet died." (The whole story is in Jeremiah 28.)

It's no small thing to claim to speak for God. But those of us who hear are responsible to evaluate a prophet's message according to the standard of God's Word. The Bible says we are to test the spirits, not trust the spirits (1 John 4:1 – 3). Jesus said that in the final judgment of human beings, some people will say, "Lord, *in your name* we prophesied and did great miracles," and Jesus will say, "I never knew you — I never had a relationship with you — get out of my sight!" (see Matthew 7:22 – 23).

Jesus has the final word on all this:

> Not everyone who says to me, "Lord, Lord" will enter the kingdom of heaven, but only he who does the will of my Father who is in heaven.
>
> Matthew 7:21

Who Were These Guys?

In Bible times, God selected certain men and women to speak his message. They didn't cook up their own message; they spoke God's truth even when no one was willing to listen. Those messengers who spoke about future events were called *prophets* or *prophetesses*. They spoke for someone else. They represented not a king or a wealthy businessman but the Lord God himself.

God moved some of the prophets to write down their message — and he also guided that process, so that what they wrote was exactly what

WHAT ABOUT NOSTRADAMUS?

The young lion will overcome the old
  one,
On the field of battle in a single combat;
He will put out his eyes in a cage of gold;
Two fleets one, then to die, a cruel
  death.

Michel de Notredame (1503 – 66), better known as Nostradamus, was a French physician who developed an interest in astrology and prophecy. He wrote prophetic four-line verses (like the one above) and arranged them in ten books of one hundred verses each. His book, titled *Centuries,* claims to predict events from his time to the year 3797.

The verses are not in chronological order. They jump back and forth throughout history, supposedly prophesying events at different points in time. His predictions, however, are couched in obscure phrases and symbols and can be interpreted pretty much according to the whims of the reader. Nostradamus

further complicates matters by not dating any of his prophecies. When the two World Trade Center towers were attacked and collapsed in September of 2001, supporters of Nostradamus found what they thought was a clear prediction of that event in one line that read, "The twins will fall." Most of Nostradamus's predictions "fit" only after the event when a suitable line or two of his writings can be pulled out and applied to the situation. James Randi, author of *The Mask of Nostradamus,* claims that in the 103 cases in which Nostradamus specifically mentions identifiable persons or dates, he was wrong 100 percent of the time!

Nostradamus reflected the secularism of the French Renaissance. Before his time, almost all end-times thinkers had expected that God would bring an end to the world. Nostradamus focused on a secular end to human history. He thought humankind would wipe itself out by war or disease. Nostradamus never spoke of divine judgment, heaven, or hell.

God wanted written. In both the Old Testament and the New Testament, prophets spoke God's message about the future.

Sometimes the prophets spoke about *their own immediate future*. God would tell the prophet which side would win a battle or what judgment would fall on a disobedient king. Good news or bad news, the prophet had to speak God's message. In 2 Chronicles 20 the Spirit of the Lord came upon Jahaziel (ja-**haz**-ee-el), and he told the king of Judah that the armies of Judah would be victorious in battle against an invading army that vastly outnumbered them (2 Chronicles 20:14 – 17). The next day the warriors of Judah found the invading army dead (20:22 – 26).

Most of the time prophets were not sent on such exciting missions. Usually the prophets spoke words of judgment. David was Israel's greatest king, but he had committed adultery and then plotted murder to keep his sin a secret. (The story is told in 2 Samuel 11.) God sent Nathan the prophet to David to tell him that God had seen the whole thing. David repented and asked God's forgiveness, but Nathan told him what God's judgment would be. The baby born out of David's adultery would die (2 Samuel 12:13 – 18).

At other times the prophets predicted *events that were fulfilled hundreds of years later*. Isaiah lived seven centuries before Jesus was born, and yet, under God's direction, Isaiah painted a vivid portrait of Jesus' death on the cross for our sins (Isaiah 53). Daniel predicted the conquests of Alexander the Great, even though Alexander was born more than two hundred years later and thousands of miles from where Daniel lived (Daniel 8:5 – 8).

Some of the predictions of biblical prophets have *yet to happen*. Isaiah pictured a world of peace in which the wolf and the lamb will lie down together and children will play safely near a cobra's den (Isaiah 11:6 – 9). Amos predicted a time of such prosperity on earth that people gathering food from a field one day will be followed by people planting a new crop the next day (Amos 9:11). John in the New Testament says that God in judgment will hurl "something like a huge mountain, all ablaze" into the sea, and a third of the sea will turn to blood (Revelation 8:8 – 9). If the predictions about David's baby and about Alexander the Great actually happened just as the prophets said they would, we can also conclude that these predictions about the future will happen exactly as the prophets said they would.

PROPHETESS PREDICTS KENNEDY ASSASSINATION

During the 1960s and 1970s Jeane Dixon became a legend, primarily because she had predicted in *Parade* magazine in 1950 that John F. Kennedy would be elected president and then would die in office. She was hailed as a clairvoyant — a person who could see clearly into the future.

But here are some of her other predictions:

- World War III would start in 1954 (wrong).
- Russia would be the first nation to land humans on the moon; China would join the United Nations in 1959; Richard Nixon would not resign as president (three more wrongs).

- Jackie Kennedy would never remarry — she married Aristotle Onassis the day after Dixon's prediction (oops).
- The Vietnam War would end in 1966 (it ended in 1975 — wrong again).

In the mid-60s, Dixon predicted that a child had been born somewhere in the Middle East on February 5, 1962, shortly after 7:00 A.M. — a child who would revolutionize the world's religions and political structure by 1999. At first Dixon said this child was a new Messiah; later she decided the child was the Antichrist.

Some Wisdom for the Journey

Prophecy in the Bible is not easy reading. Some of it is pretty difficult to read and even more difficult to understand — and only *God* has all the answers on some passages. But there are a few guidelines for finding your way around. These basic principles will help you keep your feet on solid ground as you launch out on this journey through biblical prophecy. If you ever get lost, come back to these home base coordinates on the map. They will always lead you back to safe ground.

Always Read a Prophetic Statement in the Context in Which It Was Given

Look around when you read prophecy. Ask some questions:

- Who is speaking?
- Who is listening?
- Is the prophecy about those listening or about someone else?
- What hints are there in the passage about the time frame of the prophecy?

Predictions taken out of their setting can be dangerous! In the first chapter of Acts, Jesus made a prediction. He said, "Do not leave Jerusalem, but wait for the gift my Father promised, which you have heard me speak about. For John baptized with water, but in a few days you will be baptized with the Holy Spirit" (Acts 1:4 – 5).

Does that mean that we have to travel to Jerusalem to receive the Holy Spirit? We would say, No, not at all. Why? Because Jesus (the speaker) was talking to his closest followers (those listening) about an event that would directly affect them. Jesus even says that this event will happen "in a few days" (time hint). We also know that a few days later the Holy Spirit came on Jesus' followers in power. We can read the whole story in Acts 2 — and that leads to our next principle for understanding predictions in the Bible.

Find Out What Other Scripture Passages Say about the Same Event or Person

By reading Acts 2 we know when Jesus' prediction to his disciples about the Holy Spirit was fulfilled. (That's the language, by the way, that is most often used to refer to biblical prophecies that have already happened. We say, "That prophecy or prediction was *fulfilled* when the disciples were filled with the Holy Spirit in Acts 2.")

In 2 Thessalonians 2, the apostle Paul talks about a lawless man who will be revealed in the future:

> Don't let anyone deceive you in any way, for that day will not come until the rebellion occurs and the man of lawlessness is revealed, the

BIBLE BAD GUYS

False prophets and prophetesses you will meet in the Bible:

- Balaam (Numbers 22 – 24; 2 Peter 2:14 – 17)
- Hananiah (Jeremiah 28:1 – 17)
- Shemaiah (Jeremiah 29:24 – 32)
- Ahab (Jeremiah 29:21)
- Noadiah (Nehemiah 6:14)

- A group of false prophets (Ezekiel 13:1 – 16) and false prophetesses (Ezekiel 13:17 – 23)
- Elymas (Acts 13:6 – 8)
- A string of false prophets in the last days (Matthew 24:24)
- *The* false prophet of the future (Revelation 13:11 – 18)

man doomed to destruction. He will oppose and will exalt himself over everything that is called God or is worshiped, so that he sets himself up in God's temple, proclaiming himself to be God. (2 Thessalonians 2:3 – 4)

It's certainly clear that Paul is talking about an evil, powerful person in the future who will demand worship. A reference Bible or study Bible will indicate that Revelation 13 is a passage that will give you more insight on the identity of this person. When you read Revelation 13, this person is not called "the man of lawlessness"; he is called "the beast" — and, sure enough, he demands the worship of all those under his authority (Revelation 13:15). The passages listed in a reference or study Bible at Revelation 13 may send you to Daniel 7 or Daniel 11, where we learn even more about this future evil ruler. When we put together all that the Bible says about a person or an event, we get a much clearer picture of what's happening.

Points 2 Remember

- ☑ Prophecy is what God says about the future.

- ☑ The source of reliable information from God is the Bible.

- ☑ God spoke about the future through specially chosen men and women — prophets and prophetesses.

- ☑ God has given us guidelines for discerning who are true prophets and who are false prophets.

- ☑ As difficult as prophecy may seem at times, a few crucial guidelines will keep us on track.

Some elements of biblical prophecy are discussed in only one passage of Scripture. The infamous number 666 representing the evil Antichrist is found only in Revelation 13:16 – 18 — nowhere else in Scripture. Other subjects are discussed in several places by different writers — like the passages about a future world ruler. Try to find all the pieces of a prediction and get the whole picture. I've tried to help you do that in this book. It's always a wise step to take in the study of prophecy.

Don't Be Turned Off or Freaked Out by Symbols and Imagery

Some people read about "a beast coming out of the sea" with "ten horns and seven heads" (Revelation 13:1) — and they close the book! They think it is too hard to fathom or too weird, and they give up. I admit some prophetic sections of the Bible are *very* hard to understand. But they are hard for everyone! Remember that the symbols are not literally true — the man referred to in Revelation 13 will not literally have seven heads balanced on his shoulders — but the symbols represent aspects of the prophecy that are literally true. The seven heads on the beast, for example, represent seven nations or political entities that form the base of the evil ruler's empire. We figure that out only by carefully reading the passage and by comparing it to other Scripture passages that talk about the same person or event.

Try to Read and Interpret Biblical Prophecy in Its Normal Sense

Obviously a seven-headed beast rising out of the sea needs some explanation beyond the literal sense of the words. We use figures of speech in our own language every day, and we fully expect that those listening will understand us. ("How was your math test today?" "It was a bear!" No explanation needed!)

The Bible uses figures of speech too — and allegories and metaphors and parables and even riddles — but be careful not to read in a hidden meaning when no hidden meaning is implied or necessary.

Take a look at this biblical statement:

> I saw thrones on which were seated those who had been given authority to judge. And I saw the souls of those who had been beheaded because of their testimony for Jesus and because of the word of God. They had not worshiped the beast or his image and had not received his mark on their foreheads or their hands. They came to life and reigned with Christ a thousand years. (Revelation 20:4)

DigginG DeEpeR

✗ Green, Joel. *How to Read Prophecy*. Downers Grove, Ill.: InterVarsity Press, 1984.

✗ Kaiser, Walter. *Back Toward the Future*. Grand Rapids: Baker, 1989.

Pretty straightforward, right? But the fact is that this verse has been the subject of a seemingly endless debate between Christians because some want to read it in its most literal sense ("Jesus will reign on earth for one thousand years"), while other Christians believe it is symbolic and so they see a spiritual meaning ("Jesus already reigns in his church for the entire age"). More on the interpretation issue in the next chapter.

Don't Forget How the Story Ends — God Wins!

Our look at biblical prophecy will lead us down some dark roads and through some dreadful forecasts. Don't lose heart! Our God is a sovereign God. He is in control. He can tell us what will happen, because he knows it all and planned it all — and he has told us how the story ends. Prophecy ultimately brings honor to God because it demonstrates his great power and the truth of his Word.

Okay, pick up all your gear. A fascinating journey lies just ahead!

CHAPTER 2

"I Will Return": Jesus' Second Coming

"I Will Return": Jesus' Second Coming

▸ Explore the "big idea" — Jesus is coming back!
▸ Read what the Bible said about Jesus hundreds of years before he was born
▸ Figure out why Christians disagree on how the future will unfold

Once you start looking seriously at prophecy, you'll be amazed at how much of the Bible refers to the future. We aren't talking about a few verses or a chapter here and there. Prophecy is spread all throughout the Bible.

One respected Bible scholar, J. Barton Payne, has calculated that there are 8,532 verses that contain predictive information. Twenty-seven percent of the Bible is prophecy! Payne further figured out that 6,641 Old Testament verses (28.5 percent) and 1,711 New Testament verses (21.5 percent) speak about future events.

The only Bible books that contain no predictions are Ruth and Song of Songs in the Old Testament and Philemon and 3 John in the New Testament. The remaining sixty-two books all include at least some prophetic material.

Some biblical books are almost totally prediction — Zephaniah (89 percent); Nahum (74 percent); Revelation (63 percent); 2 Peter (41 percent). Some of the larger books contain hundreds of verses of prophecy — Ezekiel has 821 verses that speak directly to the future (65 percent of the book); Isaiah, 754 verses (59 percent); Matthew, 278 verses (26 percent). (These calculations all come from J. Barton Payne, *Encyclopedia of Biblical Prophecy* [New York: Harper & Row, 1973].)

Prophecy is no minor theme in the Bible. If God put that much in his book, it's clear he wants us to know this stuff!

Jesus certainly took prophecy seriously. He repeatedly pointed to events in his ministry as the fulfillment of Old Testament predictions. When Jesus told his followers that one of them would betray him, he gave this explanation: "I am not referring to all of you; I know those I have chosen. But this is to fulfill the scripture: He who shares my bread has lifted up his heel against me" (John 13:18).

Jesus took his own predictions seriously — and he expected his followers would do so as well. He said, "I am telling you now before it happens, so that when it does happen you will believe that I am He" (John 13:19).

The Bible contains approximately 2,500 predictions about events that were future when the predictions were recorded or spoken. Two thousand of these predictions have been fulfilled in every detail. (What are the odds?) We can conclude that five hundred predictions in the Bible are about events yet to happen.

Prophecy's Big Picture

With all this material to cover, where do we start? Some people want to jump right in by talking about the mark of the beast or how long the Tribulation will last or who the Antichrist is. (If you aren't familiar with those terms, don't panic! We'll get there eventually.) As fascinating as some of those subjects are, the place to begin is with the central, most important, most universally known prediction in the Bible:

Jesus said, "I will come back" (John 14:3).

That's the bottom line of everything we believe about the future. All other prophecy revolves around and springs from this clear prediction

---

Revelation 1:3

Blessed is the one who reads the words of this prophecy, and blessed are those who hear it and take to heart what is written in it, because the time is near.

Wow! God promises a special blessing to those who study Bible prophecy!

that Jesus who lived here on earth, died on the cross, and rose from the dead — this same Jesus — will come back again.

For Christians, Jesus is everything. So we aren't surprised that, as God unfolds his future plans, Jesus is at the very center of it all.

It didn't just start in the New Testament either. It has always been the case that biblical prophecy centered around Jesus. In the Old Testament, God's prophets spoke about a great Deliverer who would come — an anointed King, the Messiah. But as those prophets looked ahead in time and saw the coming Messiah, they only saw part of the picture.

On one hand, the prophets predicted the coming of a suffering Messiah — a meek, humble servant of God who would take on himself the penalty of sin. At other times, the prophets spoke about a powerful, victorious Messiah who would conquer his enemies and rule the world. Sometimes both elements were woven into the same prophecy — like this one, for example:

> For to us a child is born,
>   to us a son is given,
>   and the government will be on his shoulders.
> And he will be called
>   Wonderful Counselor, Mighty God,
>   Everlasting Father, Prince of Peace.
> Of the increase of his government and peace
>   there will be no end.
> He will reign on David's throne
>   and over his kingdom,
> establishing and upholding it
>   with justice and righteousness
>   from that time on and forever. (Isaiah 9:6 – 7)

Isaiah (who lived seven hundred years before Jesus) saw a child born (meek and humble) who would sit on King David's throne and reign forever (powerful and victorious).

Zechariah (four hundred years before Jesus) predicted the arrival of a gentle Messiah:

> Rejoice greatly, O Daughter of Zion!
>   Shout, Daughter of Jerusalem!

> See, your king comes to you,
> > righteous and having salvation,
> > gentle and riding on a donkey,
> > on a colt, the foal of a donkey. (Zechariah 9:9)

Then, in the very next verse, the prophet says this:

> He will proclaim peace to the nations.
> > His rule will extend from sea to sea
> > and from the River to the ends of the earth. (Zechariah 9:10b)

The predictions about the Messiah were so different that some Jewish people in the first century thought there would be *two* Messiahs — one humble and sin-bearing, the second majestic and earth-conquering. The solution was not in two Messiahs, but in two appearances of the same Messiah. The Old Testament prophets didn't realize that there would be two separate times when the Messiah would come to earth. They expected just one event.

It's like looking at a photograph of a high mountain range like the Rockies or the Himalayas. Two mountain peaks may look like they're right next to each other or even part of the same mountain. When you get to the top, however, or fly over in an airplane, you realize that what looked like one peak was really two peaks separated by a long valley. As the Old Testament prophets looked ahead to the Messiah, they saw his glory and his humility displayed in one appearance. When Jesus came, however, we saw only the humble teacher, the gentle shepherd, the healer, the sin-bearer. Jesus' promise (and this cleared up the mystery) was that he would come again a second time, and this second appearance would be in awesome power.

Messiah

Techno-Speak

The word *Messiah* in Hebrew means "the Anointed One." It is a title for Jesus that is used in relation to the people of Israel. Jesus is God's great Deliverer who would deliver Israel (and all who would believe in him) from the condemnation of sin through his sacrifice on the cross. He would also deliver Israel from all her enemies through his conquering power. The New Testament (Greek) term for Messiah is *the Christ*. Jesus is his name; Christ is his title. The term *messianic prophecy* refers to Old Testament predictions about the Messiah.

Double Reference

The term *double reference* is used to describe a Scripture passage in which part of the passage is fulfilled at one time while another part is fulfilled at a later time. Zechariah 9:9 – 10 is a clear example. Verse 9 was fulfilled during Jesus' earthly ministry; verse 10 will be fulfilled at Jesus' second coming.

When Jesus was on trial in front of the Jewish authorities, the high priest challenged Jesus with these words: "I charge you under oath by the living God: Tell us if you are the Christ [Messiah], the Son of God." Jesus' reply rocked these men's hearts: "Yes, it is as you say.... But I say to all of you: *In the future* you will see the Son of Man sitting at the right hand of the Mighty One and coming on the clouds of heaven" (Matthew 26:63 – 64, emphasis added).

Jesus didn't look like the Messiah as he stood there in his carpenter's clothes, under arrest, betrayed by Judas, abandoned by his disciples. Even though all these circumstances were predicted of the Messiah in the Old Testament, these Jewish leaders were looking for a king. Jesus made it clear that the "King" part would take place "in the future." Jesus even quoted an Old Testament prediction about the Messiah (he took his words from Daniel 7:13) so these Jewish scholars wouldn't miss the point. When the members of the Council heard Jesus' words, however, they went crazy, tearing their clothes and smacking Jesus around. They never entertained the possibility that Jesus' words were true.

The "two peaks of the mountain" analogy applies to Jesus' second coming, too. Some New Testament references to the future return of Jesus read as though everything will happen as one big event. But as the New Testament was completed and as God's plan unfolded, we began to realize that Jesus' second coming had two phases to it. Jesus would return in the air for his people — that's phase one. Then Jesus would return to the earth with his people — that's phase two. We call phase one "the rapture of the church" (this topic gets a whole chapter later in the book); we call phase two "the return of Christ." Some Christians think the rapture and the return are two events separated in time (like Jesus' first coming and second coming); other Christians think both phases will occur as one grand event. But two distinct phases of Jesus' second coming are clearly evident in the Bible.

What We Learn from Jesus' First Coming

I've spent some time talking about Jesus' first coming as a baby in Bethlehem because looking at the Old Testament prophecies about Jesus' first coming will help us understand how to interpret the Old and New Testament prophecies about his second coming.

For example, the Old Testament prophet Isaiah predicted that the Messiah would be born of a woman who was a virgin. Here's the prophecy written seven hundred years before Jesus came:

> Therefore the Lord himself will give you a sign: The virgin will be with child and will give birth to a son, and will call him Immanuel. (Isaiah 7:14)

In his Gospel, Matthew tells us that a man named Joseph was absolutely devastated when he discovered that his sweet bride-to-be named Mary was pregnant. He was devastated because he knew that *he* was not the child's father, and he could only conclude that Mary had been unfaithful to him. Then an angel came to Joseph and said, "Mary has *not* been unfaithful. The child has been conceived in her by a miracle of God" (see Matthew 1:18 – 21).

Then Matthew adds this explanation:

> All this took place to fulfill what the Lord had said through the prophet: "The virgin will be with child and will give birth to a son, and they will call him Immanuel" — which means, "God with us." (Matthew 1:22 – 23)

Here's how it works:

- The prophet made a prediction that the Messiah would be born of a woman who was a virgin.
- Seven hundred years later Jesus was conceived in and born of a virgin.
- The New Testament ties the event in Jesus' life to the prediction in the Old Testament.

The prophecy was accurately fulfilled, just as the prophet said it would be.

Another example: The prophet Micah said that the Messiah would be born in Bethlehem, the same village where King David had been born.

> But you, Bethlehem Ephrathah,
>   though you are small among the clans of Judah,
> out of you will come for me
>   one who will be ruler over Israel,
> whose origins are from of old,
>   from ancient times. (Micah 5:2)

Fast-forward seven hundred years (Micah lived at the same time as the prophet Isaiah). Mary and Joseph live in Nazareth (seventy miles from Bethlehem — a long way when you had to walk!), but a taxation decree comes down from the Roman White House at precisely the right time to force Joseph and Mary to travel to Bethlehem in time for Jesus' birth.

Both Matthew and Luke tell us about Bethlehem (you hear Luke 2:4 – 6 read every Christmas), but Matthew makes a very important connection. When the Magi from the east show up in Jerusalem looking for the newly born king of the Jews, jealous King Herod calls in the Jewish brain trust and asks them where, according to prophecy, the Messiah would be born. They don't even have to check their notes! They say, "In Bethlehem! Because that is what the prophet said" — and they quote the prophecy from Micah (Matthew 2:3 – 6).

Different prophecy, same point:

• The prophet made a prediction that the Messiah would be born in Bethlehem.
• Seven hundred years later Jesus was born in Bethlehem.
• The New Testament writers link the event in Jesus' life with the Old Testament prediction.

The point I want you to see is that the Old Testament predictions were fulfilled *exactly* as the prophets said they would be fulfilled — and that's just two examples! Here's a list you can check out for yourself:

OLD TESTAMENT PROPHECIES FULFILLED LITERALLY

Prophecy about Messiah	Old Testament Prediction	Fulfillment in Jesus
Would live in Egypt awhile	Hosea 11:1	Matthew 2:15
Filled with God's Spirit	Isaiah 11:2	Luke 4:18 – 19
Would be a healer	Isaiah 53:4	Matthew 8:16 – 17
Would teach using parables	Isaiah 6:9 – 10	Matthew 13:10 – 15
His own people would reject him	Psalm 69:8; Isaiah 53:3	John 1:11; 7:5
Enter Jerusalem on a donkey	Zechariah 9:9	Matthew 21:4 – 5
Betrayed by a friend for thirty pieces of silver	Psalm 41:9; 55:12 – 14; Zechariah 11:12 – 13	Matthew 26:14 – 16, 21 – 25
Abandoned by his disciples	Zechariah 13:7	Matthew 26:31
Beaten and treated cruelly	Isaiah 50:6	Matthew 26:67; 27:26
Hands and feet pierced	Psalm 22:16; Zechariah 12:10	John 19:37
Soldiers gamble for garments	Psalm 22:18	Matthew 27:35; John 19:23 – 24
No bones broken	Psalm 34:20	John 19:33 – 36
Crucified between two thieves	Isaiah 53:12	Matthew 27:38; Mark 15:27 – 28; Luke 22:37
Buried with the rich	Isaiah 53:9	Matthew 27:57 – 60
Would rise from the dead	Psalm 16:10	Matthew 28:2 – 7; Acts 2:31 – 32

All of these prophecies were fulfilled *literally* — that is, the events happened just as each prophet said they would.

A few Old Testament prophecies were fulfilled in a more allegorical sense. For example, Herod ordered the execution of all the babies in Bethlehem. It was a cruel attempt to get rid of Jesus, but Matthew tells us that the event fulfilled a prophecy from Jeremiah:

Then what was said through the prophet Jeremiah was fulfilled:

"A voice is heard in Ramah,
    weeping and great mourning,

Rachel weeping for her children
    and refusing to be comforted,
because they are no more." (Matthew 2:17 – 18)

In Jeremiah 31:15 (where we read this prophecy), nothing is said or hinted at about the Messiah. God directed Matthew to see this prophecy as fulfilled in the sorrow in *Bethlehem,* but the prophecy itself mentions *Ramah,* a different city. So we have to conclude that occasionally a prophecy may be fulfilled in a less than literal sense as an illustration or spiritual picture of an event.

Back to the Future

This whole study of the prophecies fulfilled at Jesus' first coming gives us incredible insight when we begin to look at the prophecies about Jesus' second coming. We can expect, for example, that the majority of these prophecies will be fulfilled literally. When Jesus said, "They will see the Son of Man coming on the clouds of the sky" (Matthew 24:30), we can conclude that Jesus will actually return bodily to the earth. Our conclusion is confirmed in every New Testament promise about Jesus' return. When Jesus ascended into heaven forty days after his resurrection, two angels told the disciples, "This same Jesus, who has been taken from you into heaven, will come back in the same way you have seen him go into heaven" (Acts 1:11). The apostle Paul told the Thessalonians that they were to "wait for [God's] Son from heaven" and that "the Lord himself will come down from heaven" (1 Thessalonians 1:10; 4:16).

Jesus is not coming again in just some spiritual, allegorical sense. He is literally, visibly returning from heaven. He didn't come again in the hearts of his disciples or come in some mystical sense at another time in history. Jesus' second coming is still future. These prophecies and promises still await their fulfillment.

So Why Don't Christians Agree on Future Events?

If you talk to Christian friends or pick up a few books on biblical prophecy, it won't take you long to figure out that there are several views on how the future will unfold. The disagreements don't arise so much from what the Bible actually says but from how various traditions approach biblical prophecy as a whole.

One camp of Christians takes a literal approach to prophecy. The Old Testament predictions about the Messiah that were not fulfilled in Jesus' first coming will be fulfilled at Jesus' second coming — and just as literally as the prophecies of his first coming. For example, since the Old Testament promises the nation of Israel that the Messiah will reign in Jerusalem over a worldwide Kingdom of peace, these Christians believe that the Kingdom is still future. There will be a literal, physical Kingdom, and Jesus will reign over the earth as King.

Other Christians take a different approach. These Christians contend that, because Israel rejected Jesus as her Messiah, those Old Testament prophecies have been transferred from Israel to the church, the New Testament people of God. Therefore, we are not to look for an earthly, literal Kingdom, as Old Testament Israel did. Those promises are now fulfilled spiritually in Jesus Christ and in the church. Jesus reigns right now as King over his church and in the hearts of his people. In this view, prophecy is not to be taken so literally. Look instead for the spiritual meaning.

Still other Christians say that prophecy is to be interpreted in the context of the ongoing conflict between good and evil. The symbols of prophetic visions should not be linked to specific world events, but instead they show us that Christ will ultimately triumph over all his foes. Instead of wrangling about whether there is an earthly Kingdom or not, we should be living each day under Christ's lordship. Instead of trying to figure out who the evil Antichrist is or when he will appear, we should be trying to find new methods to proclaim the truth about the real Christ.

Within the Christian community all of these approaches (and combinations of approaches) exist and even thrive. No wonder we don't agree! Books are written, seminars are held, sermons are preached — all defending one position or another. In this book I will try to give you honest, fair exposure to all the major views. I have my own specific position, but I also want you to listen to and learn from other perspectives.

A Few Ground Rules

Several principles will help us keep our focus when it comes to the debate over how biblical prophecy should be interpreted.

Have a Position

God has given us a lot of information about the future, and he wants us to know it and believe it. It's not enough to say, "Everything will work out in the end somehow. God has it all under control." If that were God's attitude, he would have said just that much in his Word and left out all the prophetic detail! Instead God gave us his plan for the future for our understanding and encouragement.

Hold Your Own Position with Humility

The fact is that no matter what position you or I take on end-times events, Bible-believing, Christ-honoring Christians have held other views. None of us has all the answers! Keep an open mind and be willing to listen to other Christians.

Keep Discussions on the Level of Issues Rather Than Personalities

Every end-times position has some people associated with it who are rude or fanatical. All sides in the debate manage to attract people who go beyond the boundaries of Scripture to set dates or to make dogmatic pronouncements. If you focus only on the personalities, the debate will simply generate a lot of heat and very little light — friction but minimal understanding. By keeping the focus on Scripture and on the issues, we will begin to learn from each other and reject the extreme views that often bring such disgrace on the Christian community.

Quotation Marks

"There is simply no place in the family of God for name-calling, false accusation, slander, evil insinuations, and guilt-by-association techniques. God forgive us all of such sins."

Robert Lightner, in *Last Days Handbook*
(Nashville: Nelson, 1997), 131

Cultivate a Big Perspective, and Focus on What All Christians Hold in Common about Future Events

Christians who honor the Bible as God's truth have at least six broad areas of agreement when it comes to God's plan for the future.

1. *God created human beings to live forever.* Christians believe that human beings live on beyond the point of physical death. The body may die, but the human spirit or soul lives on. We are not absorbed into the universe. We do not experience reincarnation as a different form of life. Human beings were designed to be immortal — we continue to live after death.

2. *Human beings experience conscious existence between physical death and the resurrection of the body.* Christians believe that at death those people who have believed in Jesus in this life enter a state of rest and joy in the presence of Jesus. Those who have refused to believe in Jesus enter a state of separation from him. Human beings are consciously aware of where they are and what is going on around them.

Points 2 Remember

☑ More than one-quarter of the Bible is prophecy.

☑ The bottom-line prophecy is that *Jesus will return.*

☑ Based on how the predictions about Jesus' first coming were fulfilled, we can expect the majority of the prophecies about Jesus' second coming to be fulfilled literally.

☑ Christians agree on the big issues about the future. We disagree on the time sequence of events or on how prophecy overall is to be interpreted.

3. *The bodies of human beings will be raised from the dead.* All human beings, whether believers or unbelievers, will be raised from the dead. Our conscious spirits will in the future be reunited with our resurrected bodies. The bodies of believers in Jesus will experience the resurrection to life. Our eternal bodies will be free from sin, pain, and disease forever. The bodies of unbelievers will experience the resurrection to condemnation. Their bodies will be raised to stand in judgment before God.

4. *All human beings will stand before God to give an account of their lives.* Unbelievers will simply hear God's sentence of eternal separation. They will be without excuse for their rejection of God's gift of salvation. Believers in Jesus will give an account too. We will have our lives evalu-

ated and rewarded according to the faithfulness of our obedience to Jesus Christ.

5. *Jesus will return.* All Christians agree that Jesus will return to earth a second time. The Bible is so clear on the *fact* of Jesus' return that there is no real debate about it.

6. *An eternal heaven is prepared for those who believe in Jesus as Savior; eternal separation from Jesus will be the destiny of those who refuse God's grace.* There is no disagreement among Christians that we will all experience eternity. We look for a new heaven and a new earth of peace and joy forever.

On the big items, all Christians are in agreement! It doesn't matter what your denomination or tradition is, these six issues make the cut every time. All Christians also agree that the Bible contains a number of prophecies that have yet to be fulfilled. We are all certain of those events. Where we disagree is with respect to the sequence and timing of those events. We debate and write books about what prophecies have been fulfilled and what prophecies remain to be fulfilled. We publish newsletters and create organizations dedicated to one particular view of how future events will unfold. This book explores more disagreements and variations than you ever imagined existed, but I urge you not to lose sight of our agreement as Christians on the big issues. This doesn't mean we shouldn't hold and defend a particular position, but it does put our disagreements into proper perspective.

Some day God will do his work of bringing human history to an end and we will all agree on one more issue: We will all say that God was right, and *all* of us to some degree were wrong.

DigginG DeEpeR

✗ Benware, Paul. *Understanding End Times Prophecy: A Comprehensive Approach.* Chicago: Moody Press, 1995.

CHAPTER 3

Terror at Every Turn:
The Tribulation

Terror at Every Turn: The Tribulation

Heads Up

▸ The future never looked so bad!

▸ Find out if the worst of God's judgment on evil people is already past — or is yet to come

▸ Don't be discouraged. God wins!

Movies have a way of scaring us to death! Sitting in a dark theater you can almost believe the erupting volcanoes that swallow cities or the alien invasions or the nuclear missile attacks. What might surprise you is that some day some of the worst scenes you can imagine will actually happen. The world is headed for disaster — not a disaster initiated by human beings, but a day of judgment from God. This period of distress and chaos is called the Tribulation.

The word *tribulation* is used in the Bible in a general sense to mean "troubles" (1 Corinthians 7:28), "suffering" (Acts 7:11), "anguish" (John 16:21), and "hardships" (Acts 14:22). But the word is also used to describe a specific time of distress that God will bring on the world. Jesus said, "For then there will be great distress, unequaled from the beginning of the world until now — and never to be equaled again" (Matthew 24:21). The book of Revelation pictures men and women who are violently killed for their faith during a time called "the great tribulation" (Revelation 7:14). Other descriptions of the Tribulation emphasize that God's judgment will be severe and intense. No one will escape.

The Bible talks about the Tribulation in several places — in the Old Testament books of Daniel, Zechariah, and Zephaniah and in the New Testament Gospels and in Paul's Letters. The book of Revelation devotes more than half its pages to a description of what the Tribulation will be like. The apostle John (the author of Revelation) didn't just read about those events; he saw them leap to life right in front of his

A TRIBULATION BY ANY OTHER NAME

Here are some of the terms and phrases used in the Bible to refer to the Tribulation:

Jeremiah 30:7	A time of trouble for Jacob
Zephaniah 1:14 – 16	The great day of the Lord
	A day of wrath
	A day of distress and anguish
	A day of trouble and ruin
	A day of darkness and gloom
	A day of clouds and blackness
	A day of trumpet and battle cry
Zephaniah 1:18	The day of the Lord's wrath
	The fire of the Lord's jealousy
Isaiah 34:8	A day of vengeance
Daniel 9:24 – 27	The final "seven"
Daniel 12:1	A time of distress such as has not happened from the beginning of nations until then
Joel 1:15	Destruction from the Almighty
Malachi 4:5	The great and dreadful day of the Lord
Matthew 24:8	Birth pains
1 Thessalonians 1:10	The coming wrath
Revelation 3:10	The hour of trial that is going to come on the whole world
Revelation 6:17	The great day of God's wrath

eyes. John "saw" the future unfold, and then he wrote down what he saw so we could "see" it too.

John saw the events of the future in a vision. Think about the most vivid dream you've ever had, and then imagine that you were awake as you saw the events unfold. John was not dreaming all this up, of course. God was giving the vision to John, and even guiding John as he wrote it down, so that we now have an accurate record of the vision.

John didn't see the events in Revelation like we see events on a CNN news clip. John's visions are filled with symbols and images. Sometimes the images are identified, and sometimes they aren't. For example, instead of seeing pictures of starving people lined up at a United Nations' feeding station, John sees a black horse ride out onto the world stage. The rider of the horse carries a pair of scales in his hand. A voice then announces that a small handful of wheat will cost a whole day's paycheck (Revelation 6:5 – 6). It's obviously a picture of famine sweeping the world, but John sees it in dramatic images.

God uses the images to make a powerful impression on John and on John's readers. It's one thing to read that an evil ruler will one day dominate the world; it's quite another thing to see an enormous beast with seven heads rise out of the sea and conquer the world (Revelation 13:1 – 10). You might yawn through a recitation of simple words, but you won't be able to get an image like that out of your mind.

The images are not just John's unique way of jazzing up the story. Images represent real events or real people. The seven-headed beast represents an evil ruler — the Antichrist. The black horse and its rider represent a real famine that will actually happen. Many of the symbols and images in Revelation can be identified by referring to hints in the text or by reading other passages of Scripture. A few of the images have baffled Christians for centuries.

Christians agree that the Tribulation is real; what they don't agree on is *when* the Tribulation will come. You may have been taught one particular view of the Tribulation, and you may be convinced that your view is correct. The reality is that other persons who are just as committed as you are to an accurate interpretation of the Bible have proposed other perspectives.

Views of the Tribulation

Three main views of the Tribulation have emerged in the Christian community. I'll attempt to explain each view and give the arguments for each. When you examine all the possibilities, you might find your own position strengthened — or changed.

Possibility #1: The Tribulation Is Past

Some Christians believe that the predictions in the New Testament about a time of great distress were fulfilled very soon after they were written. In their view, the Tribulation is not some future period of time, but a series of events that happened in the past — about forty years after Jesus' death and resurrection.

In A.D. 70 the armies of the Roman Empire crushed a Jewish rebellion in Judea, the land where Jesus had lived. The Romans devastated the land, killed hundreds of thousands of Jews, and leveled the city of Jerusalem. The Temple where Jesus had taught (called the Second Temple or Herod's Temple) was burned to the ground. The massive stones of the city walls were pulled down. Jerusalem looked like a bombed-out, burned-out wasteland.

This destruction was God's judgment on Israel for rejecting Jesus as her promised Messiah. Some persons in Israel had believed in Jesus, but the nation as a whole, along with her religious leadership, had refused to accept him. The "tribulation" of the Roman attack was God's way of showing everyone that the old way of worship and the old order of the Law had ended. God was now offering his grace through the new way of faith in Jesus alone.

In Our Defense

Those who hold the view that the Tribulation occurred in the past base their position on the following biblical teachings:

• Jesus, in a long sermon about the future, tells his followers about Tribulation events — wars and rumors of wars, famines, earthquakes, betrayals, false Christs. Jesus even refers to the coming time as "tribulation" or "distress" (Matthew 24:21, 29). Then Jesus adds,

Techno-Speak

Preterist

The position that the Tribulation happened in the past is called the *preterist* view. The term comes from the Latin word *praeteritus,* which means "gone by" or "past." Some prominent Christian leaders who have held this view are Origen (185 – 254), Eusebius (260 – 340), John Calvin (1509 – 1564), and Matthew Henry (1662 – 1714). The preterist view of the Tribulation is usually held by those who are also *amillennial* or *postmillennial* in their view of the Kingdom. (See chapter 7 for more details on Kingdom views.) The Christian Reconstructionist movement also advocates a preterist view of the Tribulation. The main contemporary defenders of the "tribulation is past" view are R. C. Sproul, Kenneth Gentry, Gary DeMar, and David Chilton.

Olivet Discourse

Jesus' sermon about the future is called the "Olivet discourse" because he spoke the sermon on the Mount of Olives, a hill just east of the city of Jerusalem. The sermon was given late in Jesus' ministry, shortly before his arrest and crucifixion. Don't confuse it with the Sermon on the Mount (Matthew 5 – 7), which Jesus delivered early in his ministry. The Olivet discourse is recorded in Matthew 24 – 25, Mark 13, and Luke 21. Read it yourself!

Techno-Speak

"I tell you the truth, this generation will certainly not pass away until all these things have happened" (Matthew 24:34). Jesus was (apparently) referring to the generation of people alive at the time he spoke. So Jesus is telling his followers that the Tribulation would occur during their lifetimes — and forty years later the Tribulation came when the Roman armies smashed Jerusalem. The "this generation will certainly not pass away" statement is a key time text for this view of the Tribulation.

- The "signs" that Jesus said would point to the approach of the Tribulation were fulfilled by events in the first century. "Wars and rumors of wars" (Matthew 24:6) refer to the civil unrest in the Roman Empire at the death of Emperor Nero in A.D. 68. There was also the protracted war between the Romans and the Jews (A.D. 67 – 70). Increased "famines and earthquakes" (Matthew 24:7) occur in the years between Jesus' crucifixion and the destruction of the Temple. A massive earthquake struck Jerusalem during the first year of the war with Rome.

- Jesus' prediction that "this gospel of the kingdom will be preached in the whole world" (Matthew 24:14) was a promise that the message of Jesus would be proclaimed to the Jewish people living in the Roman "world" before the Tribulation would come. The first-century Jews had the opportunity to believe in Jesus, but the majority rejected him.

- The "abomination" that Jesus said would appear in the Temple (Matthew 24:15) refers to the Roman insignia carried by the troops. These were adorned with religious images that God specifically prohibited in Israel's worship.

- The "great tribulation" or "great distress" (Matthew 24:21) that would come on Israel was the destruction of the Temple and the permanent end of the animal sacrifices required by the Old Testament Law. Since A.D. 70 the Jewish people have not had an acceptable place of sacrifice to God.
- The "coming" of the Son of Man (Matthew 24:30) that Jesus talked about was *not* the visible physical return of Jesus but his "coming" in judgment against Israel. Jesus says that "the *sign* of the Son of Man will appear in the sky." He does not say that the Son of Man will appear.
- The destruction of Jerusalem signaled a change in God's program from a focus on the nation of Israel and the Temple to a focus on the message of Jesus for all the world. The fall of Jerusalem marked the final separation of Christianity from Judaism. The Christian community, or the church, becomes the "new Israel" in God's plan.
- Those who believe the Tribulation is past also see confirmation of their view in the New Testament book of Revelation. They assert that the apostle John received his visions during the reign of the Roman emperor Nero (A.D. 54 – 68), just before the first government-sanctioned persecution of Christians. John wrote to prepare the Christians for that time of great distress. He was also warning Christians of the coming destruction of Jerusalem and the resulting reorientation of Christianity away from Judaism.
- According to the preterist view, the book of Revelation is a highly figurative book that cannot be interpreted with simple literalism. We have to read the book as poetry or drama. John was being "shown" certain events, not "told" specifically what would happen.

A PRETERIST EXPLAINS

"I hold that the Tribulation occurred in our distant past in the first century.... I hold that the Tribulation closes out the Jewish-based, old covenant order, and establishes the new covenant (Christian) order.... Preterism holds that the tribulation prophecies occur in the first century, thus in our past."

Kenneth L. Gentry Jr., in *The Great Tribulation: Past or Future?*
(Grand Rapids: Kregel, 1999), 12 – 13

- Chapters 4 – 19 of the book of Revelation describe the Tribulation in symbolic terms, but it was all fulfilled in A.D. 70. Preterists are divided about the final return of Jesus pictured in Revelation 19. Some think that it is a symbolic portrait of Jesus acting in judgment on Israel through the Roman army; others think that the story "leaps ahead" to the still future return of Jesus in glory.
- The apostle John, the human recorder of Revelation, expected the soon fulfillment of his predictions. He repeatedly is told that he will see the things that "must soon take place" (Revelation 1:1; 2:16; 22:6, 7, 10). If we've had to wait almost 2000 years for the prophecies to be fulfilled, that's not "soon"! John wanted his original readers to understand that these predictions would be fulfilled in their lifetimes — in the events surrounding the Roman destruction of Jerusalem in A.D. 70.

On the Other Hand

Christians who hold differing views of the time of the Tribulation have raised some interesting questions about the "A.D. 70 Tribulation" position.

- The Old Testament prophets, Jesus, and the book of Revelation all make it clear that the Tribulation will end with the *rescue* of Israel and the *destruction* of the enemy armies. The exact reverse happened in A.D. 70 — Israel was crushed and the Roman armies were victorious. Therefore, the destruction of Jerusalem in A.D. 70 cannot be the predicted Tribulation. (See Zechariah 12:2 – 3, 8 – 10; Matthew 24:31; Revelation 19:11 – 21.)
- Zechariah in the Old Testament, Jesus in his sermon about the future, and John in Revelation say that the Tribulation will end with the second coming of Jesus in visible glory (Zechariah 14:2 – 12; Matthew 24:29 – 30; Revelation 19:11 – 16). To say that this "coming" refers to Jesus' coming in judgment distorts the normal meaning of the Bible's words. You can't take some of Jesus' words literally (such as, real armies surrounding the actual city of Jerusalem) and then make the rest of his words symbolic (like, his "coming" as a symbol of judgment on Israel carried out through the armies of Rome).
- Those who believe that the Tribulation is in the distant past base many of their conclusions on Jesus' sermon about the future in

Matthew 24. But Jesus' sermon also appears in the Gospels of Mark and Luke. Luke's record clearly points out the contrast between the past judgment on Israel in A.D. 70 and the future judgment on the world in the Tribulation. In Luke 21:5 – 24 Jesus refers to the destruction of Jerusalem in A.D. 70 and calls that event "the time of punishment." Jerusalem's fall is followed by the "times of the Gentiles" (verse 24) — the time when Israel is dominated by non-Jewish world powers, a time we are still in today. Then the Tribulation comes (verses 25 – 26), ending with the coming of Christ to rescue his repentant people (verses 27 – 28). Luke makes it clear that when Jerusalem is destroyed the first time, it is not the end.

- The view that the prophecies about the Tribulation were fulfilled in Judea in A.D. 70 hardly fits with the global language used in the book of Revelation to describe the catastrophic judgments of God. Even if you limit the "worldwide" language to the Roman Empire, the war against the Jews in one tiny frontier province like Judea doesn't fit the biblical language.

- Jesus' statement that "this generation will certainly not pass away until all these things have happened" (Matthew 24:34) does not have to be restricted to the generation to which Jesus was talking. He could mean that the generation alive when the final events *begin* to happen will not pass away until it has all been fulfilled.

- When John in the book of Revelation says that the events of the Tribulation will come "soon" (Revelation 1:1; 22:6), he can also mean quickly or suddenly, without warning. The term refers to the way in which the events will unfold once they start, not to the time of the Tribulation itself.

Possibility #2: The Tribulation Is Timeless

Another approach to understanding the Tribulation is called the *idealist* view. According to this perspective, the predictions in the Bible about the Tribulation represent the eternal conflict between good and evil. These conflicts exist in every period of history. The Christians who hold this view of the Tribulation argue that the symbols used in prophecy do not represent any single event in the past or in the future but themes and trends in any age. For example, the beast coming out of the sea in Revelation 13 is not a picture of a single oppressive Roman emperor like Nero (as those who believe that the Tribulation

Idealist

Most Christians who hold to the idealist approach to interpreting biblical prophecy are also *amillennial* in their view of Christ's Kingdom. (See chapter 7 for a discussion of the various Kingdom views.) They tend to interpret prophetic statements in a spiritual sense rather than in a literal sense.

is past would say), nor is it a picture of the future evil ruler called the Antichrist (as those who believe that the Tribulation is future would say). The "beast" is symbolic of oppressive political power at any time in history.

The idealist approach sees the book of Revelation and other biblical predictions about the future as allegories of Satan's constant attempts to overthrow God's sovereign authority and to persecute God's people. Prophecy is not designed to lay out the specific events of the past or the future but to speak to each generation in its own situation. Prophecy assures us that God will ultimately win!

Positive Points

Christians who hold to an idealist position defend their view by appealing more to general biblical themes than to specific statements of Scripture.

- The idealist or timeless approach allows prophecy to apply directly and powerfully to each generation of readers. If the Tribulation already happened in the first century, most of Revelation is just ancient history. If the Tribulation is still future, chapters 6 – 19 of Revelation may be significant to that future generation of readers, but those who are alive today don't profit very much. If, however, these chapters point us to timeless principles at work in every generation, then we can apply prophetic Scripture to our lives right now.
- Reading biblical prophecy as a picture of the struggle in every age between good and evil prompts us to courageous living and faithful endurance, no matter how oppressive our circumstances. We are assured that, in the end, evil will be cast down and God will triumph.

AN IDEALIST EXPLAINS

"We must resist the temptation to link each trumpet [referring to the trumpet judgments recorded in Revelation 8 – 9] with a particular date or person in history. The trumpets indicate a series of happenings or calamities that will occur again and again throughout the earthly existence of the church."

Sam Hamstra, in *Four Views on the Book of Revelation*, ed. C. Marvin Pate (Grand Rapids: Zondervan, 1998), 108

- John, the author of Revelation, even said that some Christians in his day were in tribulation or distress as he wrote (Revelation 2:9 – 10, 13) — which shows that John did not have one specific time period in mind for these prophecies but was focused instead on timeless principles.
- For John, the time between Jesus' first coming and his second coming is short. Whatever happens must shortly come to pass. So his visions deal with all of history. The visions are not meant to provide details of particular wars or plagues or earthquakes. Everything is described in general terms. These are forces that are part of the human condition all the time. The symbols of Revelation point out the distress that can come on any of us who live in an evil world. Revelation also reminds us that God still rules from his throne, even over a world in chaos.

Quality Questions

Every Christian would agree with the idealist conclusion that the assurance of God's triumph over evil is a powerful motivation to courageous allegiance to Jesus Christ. But many Christians would challenge the idealist approach to what the Bible says about the Tribulation.

- Why does God give such detailed information to us about the Tribulation if he did not intend for us to think that actual historical events were being described?
- What about the specific places mentioned in prophecy (Jerusalem, for instance) or specific periods of time (forty-two months)? Are we

to read these simply as figures of speech with a deeper "spiritual" meaning, or are we to interpret them in a normal way — the way we interpret the rest of the Bible?

- Since almost all the prophecies about Jesus' first coming were fulfilled literally, can't we conclude that the prophecies surrounding his second coming will also be fulfilled literally?

- Does Jesus return to earth in some spiritual way in every age, or will his return be an actual event sometime in the future? If Jesus' return (recorded in Revelation 19) will be an actual event (as most idealists believe), why isn't the emergence of an evil world leader (recorded in Revelation 13) an actual event in history?

Possibility #3: The Tribulation Is Future

The third view of where the Tribulation fits into God's plan for human history is called the *futurist* view. Christians who hold this view believe that the Bible's predictions about the Tribulation will be fulfilled in a time of intense judgment from God in the future.

This future seven-year period will begin when a prominent world leader signs a political treaty with Israel. This powerful political leader will promise peace and security, but the peace won't last very long. Human culture and government authority will soon begin to unravel. During the first three and a half years of the Tribulation, a succession of judgments from God will sweep over the world. War, famine, and disaster will claim millions of lives. Powerful forces of evil will gain control over human society.

WHERE'S THE EMPHASIS?

Those who believe that the Tribulation is already past put the emphasis on the original readers of the book of Revelation and the political circumstances of the first century. Those who believe that the Tribulation is a timeless parable of the conflict between good and evil emphasize the relevance of the book for present-day readers. Those who believe that the Tribulation is still future emphasize the value of knowing in advance God's plan for human history and living in the light of his ultimate victory.

A FUTURIST EXPLAINS

"I do not believe the Bible teaches that the Tribulation is in any way <u>past</u>. Instead, Scripture tells us that it is a future event that could commence very soon."

Thomas Ice, in *The Great Tribulation: Past or Future?*
(Grand Rapids: Kregel, 1999), 69

At the middle of the Tribulation, the same world leader who signed the treaty with Israel will invade Israel and enter a rebuilt Temple in Jerusalem. He will proclaim himself to be god and will demand the world's worship. This act of desecration reveals the leader to be the Antichrist.

The Jewish people will realize that the Antichrist is not a political deliverer but a betrayer. His hatred of God and of the people of Israel becomes graphically apparent when he erects an image of himself in the Temple as the object of the world's adoration. Many Jews will heed Jesus' warning and will flee into the desert of Judea, where God will protect them for the last three and a half years of the Tribulation.

Wave after wave of judgment will crash down on the world during the second half of the Tribulation. Finally the Antichrist will gather the armies of the world around Jerusalem with the intention of destroying the Jews. Jesus will then return from heaven in power and splendor to rescue surviving Israel and to destroy the Antichrist and his armies. Jesus will prepare the earth for a thousand-year reign of peace and abundance.

Speaking for the Defense

Those who are convinced that the Tribulation is a future event base their view on the following biblical information:

- This is the only view that takes a consistently literal approach to how the words of biblical prophecy are understood. Prophecy does include symbols and symbolic language, but futurists believe that the symbols represent actual events and people. For example, when

John saw 144,000 people in Revelation 7:4, futurists believe that this represents an actual group of 144,000 people. Those who hold other views have to "spiritualize" this number to represent the whole body of Christians or the Christians alive in Jerusalem in the first century. Futurists hold that the words of Scripture should be understood in their normal sense. Figures of speech are obvious in the text. If the normal sense makes sense, don't go looking for secret meanings!

- The literal approach to understanding Scripture applies to Jesus' sermon about the future, too. When Jesus said that "they will see [after the Tribulation] the Son of Man coming on the clouds of the sky, with power and great glory" (Matthew 24:30), futurists accept the statement at face value. Futurists don't have to say (as other interpreters do), "Well, that's what it says, but it *really* means that Jesus will come in judgment against Israel through the Roman armies."

- The magnitude of the prophecies about the future (the sun is darkened; one-third of the world's population is killed) suggests that these events have not yet occurred in history. Nothing in the destruction of Jerusalem in A.D. 70 or in any period of time since then corresponds to the range or severity of these biblical predictions.

- God did not *replace* the people of Israel in his program or *transfer* the Old Testament promises from Israel to the Christian church. The earthly Kingdom promised in the Old Testament was *postponed* because of Israel's rejection of Jesus as the Messiah. God, however, has not forgotten these promises. He will draw Israel to faith in Jesus during the Tribulation, and then the promise of an earthly Kingdom will be literally fulfilled when Jesus reigns in majesty for a thousand years.

Quotation Marks

THE NATION OF ISRAEL

"Few events can claim equal significance as far as Bible prophecy is concerned as that of the return of Israel to their land. It constitutes a preparation for the end of the age, the setting for the coming of the Lord for his church, and the fulfillment of Israel's prophetic destiny."

John Walvoord, in *Israel in Prophecy* (Grand Rapids: Zondervan, 1962), 26

Techno-Speak

Futurist

Most Christians who believe that the Tribulation is future are also *premillennial* in their view of the Kingdom of God. (See chapter 7 for a discussion of the Kingdom.) In their view Jesus will return to earth at the end of the Tribulation to set up a visible Kingdom on earth for a thousand years.

- According to Jesus (in Matthew 24) and the book of Revelation, the Tribulation ends with the people of Israel (Jews living in the land of Israel) coming to faith in Jesus and being rescued from the oppression of the Antichrist. In A.D. 70 the Jews in Jerusalem were slaughtered or driven out of the city. The destruction of Jerusalem in the first century could not have been the Tribulation predicted in the Bible.

I Don't Think So

Those Christians who believe that the Tribulation is past or that the Tribulation principles are at work in every generation have not let futurists off the hook when it comes to tough challenges.

- What about the repeated statements of the biblical writers that these events of the Tribulation would "soon" take place, that "the time is near"? Jesus said, "This generation will certainly not pass away until all these things have happened" (Matthew 24:34). Do futurists take these words literally? Was Jesus mistaken?
- Futurists have gone overboard on their "literal" interpretation and have missed the point. Some prophecy pundits have tried to find end-times fulfillment in every newspaper headline. Others have dissected the seven heads and ten horns of the beast, trying to figure out which world leader might be the Antichrist! The futurists have pressed the interpretation of Revelation and other prophecies too far. God wanted us to get the big picture, not microanalyze the details.
- The view that the Tribulation is future totally removes the relevance of the book of Revelation for John's original readers — and even for readers today. How can predictions about events far in the future bring comfort to people who are suffering persecution right now?

- The predictions of judgment in Revelation are not global or worldwide in scope. Most of the references to "the earth" should instead be translated "the land," meaning the land of Judea, where most of the Jews lived in the first century. These are the very people who had crucified Jesus and who had said that God's judgment for killing Jesus should fall on them and on their children (Matthew 27:25). These people are the ones who experienced the judgment of the Tribulation. It is not for some future generation at all.

Points 2 Remember

☑ The Tribulation is a time of God's intense judgment on a world that has rejected him.

☑ Christians have proposed several ways to understand how the Tribulation fits into God's plan. Some believe that the predictions about the Tribulation were fulfilled in the past when Jerusalem was destroyed by the Romans. Others believe that every generation may experience Tribulation-like conditions when Christians are oppressed and persecuted. Still other Christians are convinced that the Tribulation will come on the world in the future — a seven-year period of great distress.

☑ Christians who hold to a future Tribulation believe that the Tribulation will end with the visible return of Jesus Christ to the earth to destroy the Antichrist and to set up a Kingdom of peace on earth.

Searching for Common Ground

Each of the three views on the Tribulation is held by sincere Christians who claim that they are interpreting the Bible as God intended it to be interpreted. So which view is right? Is it possible that each view tells us only part of the story — that each one emphasizes one aspect of the truth, but not the whole truth?

Those who believe that the Tribulation happened in the first century when Jerusalem was destroyed emphasize God's powerful works of judgment in the past. But does the past tell the whole story? Maybe the past "distress" was a *prefillment* of the Bible's predictions about the Tribulation, but the *full-fillment* is yet to come in the future. God's work of judgment isn't finished yet. What Israel experienced in part in A.D. 70 will be experienced by the whole world in the future time of distress.

And while the events of the past and the predictions for the future are interesting to study, maybe we also need to let prophecy speak more directly to our lives today, as the idealists suggest. It's one thing to debate how anyone will survive the cruelty of the Antichrist; it's something else to survive persecution and slavery in Sudan today or to stand for the faith against the official opposition of the North Korean government. Those of us in western democracies find it relatively easy to relegate the book of Revelation to some future day. We forget that brothers and sisters in Christ may be experiencing the equivalent of the Tribulation right now.

Digging Deeper

The best general studies on the Tribulation are

✗ Pate, C. Marvin, ed. *Four Views on the Book of Revelation*. Grand Rapids: Zondervan, 1998.

✗ Gregg, Steve, ed. *Revelation: Four Views — A Parallel Commentary*. Nashville: Nelson, 1997.

If you want to explore the view that the Tribulation is past, start with

✗ Sproul, R. C. *The Last Days according to Jesus*. Grand Rapids: Baker, 1998.

If you prefer to investigate the idealist view of the Tribulation, check out

✗ Hendriksen, William. *More Than Conquerors: An Interpretation of the Book of Revelation*. Grand Rapids: Baker, 1944 and many reprints.

✗ Wilcock, Michael. *The Message of Revelation: I Saw Heaven Opened*. The Bible Speaks Today series. Downers Grove, Ill.: InterVarsity Press, 1975.

The future Tribulation view is presented in

✗ Walvoord, John. *End Times: Understanding Today's World Events in Biblical Prophecy*. Nashville: Word, 1998.

Comparing the Candidates

Here's how the three main Tribulation views interpret Revelation 13:

	Tribulation Is Past View	Tribulation Is Timeless View	Tribulation Is Future View
The beast coming out of the sea (verse 1)	The Roman emperor Nero rose up to persecute Christians and ordered the initial attack on Jerusalem.	Satan works through evil governments to oppress and persecute God's people in every age.	An evil political leader, the Antichrist, will emerge during the Tribulation and seek to dominate the world.
The fatal wound from which the beast recovers (verse 3)	After Nero's death, the Roman Empire was thrown into a convulsive civil war in which three emperors succeeded one another in a single year. Amazingly, the empire stabilized and survived this mortal political "wound."	Evil governments may be removed for a while, but corrupt leaders will continue to emerge at various levels to oppress Christians.	The Antichrist will suffer a physical wound that appears fatal. He will recover, however, through Satan's power. His recovery will strengthen his grip on people who are under his political authority.
The second beast emerges from the land (verses 11–15)	The Jewish leaders in Judea joined with the first beast (the Roman emperor) in an attempt to destroy the Christian church.	False religious systems will arise that encourage devotion to the state instead of devotion to God.	A false prophet will come on the scene and will lead the religious cult focused on the worship of the Antichrist.
The mark of the beast (verses 16–17)	Christians in the Roman Empire were deprived of the most basic rights and privileges during times of persecution. Roman and Jewish leaders organized economic boycotts against Christians.	The state will reward the followers of false religions with economic and political power. At the same time, Christians under persecution will not be given access to positions of power or wealth.	The false prophet will require men and women to receive a brand on their forehead or hand that will allow them to hold a job, buy food, and avoid arrest. The "mark" indicates a person's willful allegiance to the Antichrist.
666 (verse 18)	The first-century spelling of Nero Caesar's name, written in Hebrew characters, adds up to 666.	This is a code name John uses to label false religion. Humankind's religion may look perfect, but it falls short of God's desire. The number 666 is a symbol of failure before God.	The number represents the name of the Antichrist. It is unclear to us what it means precisely, but at that time it will be obvious to those who are experiencing the events.
The image of the beast (verses 14–15)	The image of the beast refers to the images of Caesar and other religious symbols that were carried on the Roman standards. These images desecrated the Temple of God.	Governments will set up elaborate structures to impress those who will follow their lead and to oppress the true people of God.	The Antichrist will enter the Temple in Jerusalem and proclaim himself to be god. He will allow an image of himself to be set up as the object of the world's worship.

HELP FILE

SEVENTY SETS OF SEVEN (OR WHAT DANIEL DID WITH SEVENTY WEEKS)

Six hundred years before Jesus was born, a young boy was taken from his home in Jerusalem and brought to Babylon, the capital of a great empire. Daniel resisted incredible pressure to compromise his faith in the true God, and eventually he became a prophet, God's spokesman to the political movers and shakers of his day. Other deportations from Judea to Babylon followed until almost the entire population of the Jews was held captive.

One day, as Daniel was reading the writings of another prophet, Jeremiah, he realized that God had predicted the release of the people at the end of seventy years of captivity. Daniel thought that when the people returned to Jerusalem, God would at last restore to the Jews a glorious Kingdom. They would experience a golden age like the days of David and Solomon five hundred years earlier. God sent an angel, Gabriel, to tell Daniel that Israel would have to wait longer than seventy years for the promised Kingdom. They would have to pass through "seventy 'sevens' " (most often understood as seventy times seven years, seventy "weeks" of years, or 490 years) before the

Kingdom would begin. (The prophecy is in Daniel 9:24 – 27.)

The event that would start the clock ticking on the 490 years was a decree to rebuild and restore the city of Jerusalem. The "seventy 'sevens' " are then divided into three sections.

Division 1: Seven "Sevens" (Forty-nine Years)

A couple of possibilities exist for the decree that began the prophetic calculation. Most scholars take the decree of Artaxerxes that allowed Nehemiah to rebuild Jerusalem in 445 B.C. as the beginning of the 490-year clock (Nehemiah 2:1). Forty-nine years later (around 400 B.C.), the last prophet to speak for God in the Old Testament made his appearance in Jerusalem. After Malachi died, no prophet would speak to Israel until John the Baptizer came to them four hundred years later.

Division 2: Sixty-two "Sevens" (434 Years)

The second division of years in God's prophecy to Daniel spanned sixty-two "sevens," or 434 years. The forty-nine years of division

1 and the 434 years of division 2 bring the people of Judah to the time of Jesus' public ministry. God adds this fact in Daniel 9:26: "After the sixty-two 'sevens,' the Anointed One [Messiah] will be cut off and will have nothing."

God told his people exactly when the Messiah would come — and he told them more than 500 years before Jesus' birth. God also implied that there would be an interval of time between the second division of the prophecy (sixty-two weeks) and the third division (the seventieth week). The Messiah would be cut off, that is, violently killed, *after* the first 489 years. God also said that Jerusalem would be destroyed — an event that happened forty years after Jesus was crucified — another "gap" of time between division 2 and division 3.

Division 3: The Final "Week" of Years (Seven Years)

Christians have different views about where the seventieth "week" fits into God's program. Some say that after Jesus died and rose again, the Kingdom of God was established on earth through the Christian church. National Israel had rejected the Messiah, so God chose a "new" Israel to populate his Kingdom.

Other Christians believe that the interval before the final period of seven years is still continuing today. National Israel rejected Jesus as the Messiah. As a result, the

DID GOD'S PREDICTIONS COME TRUE?

Here are the predicted events from Daniel 9:24 – 27 that have already happened:

- A decree was issued to rebuild Jerusalem (Nehemiah 2:7 – 8).
- The people of Israel were released from Babylon, and many returned to Jerusalem (Ezra 1:1 – 5).
- The Temple was rebuilt (Ezra 6:15 – 17).
- The city walls were rebuilt (Nehemiah 6:15 – 16).
- A time period of 483 years passed between the decree to rebuild the city and the coming of the Messiah.
- The Messiah came to Israel and offered her the Kingdom, but he was violently killed (Matthew 4:17; 21:9 – 11; 27:35).

- Jerusalem was destroyed in A.D. 70 by the Roman armies.
- The Temple was also destroyed and has not been rebuilt.

Many Christians believe that these predictions from Daniel 9:24 – 27 remain to be fulfilled in the future:

- The Antichrist will come on the scene and make a covenant with Israel.
- The Temple in Jerusalem will be rebuilt for the third time.
- Animal sacrifices will begin but will be halted by the Antichrist's intervention.
- The Antichrist will commit an abomination (horrible deed) in the Temple.
- The end will come through a flood of war and destruction.

promised Kingdom was *postponed,* not transferred to the Christian church. The Church Age has intervened for two thousand years, but when the church (the true followers of Jesus) is taken out of the world at the rapture, the clock will start ticking again on the final seven years. The "seventieth week" of Daniel will be the seven years of the Tribulation. God will focus again on national Israel and will bring Israel to faith in her true Messiah. At the end of the seven years, Jesus will return in visible glory and will set up his Kingdom on earth.

The prophecy in Daniel even talks about Tribulation events. God says that a ruler (political leader) will make a covenant with many for one "seven" — one period of seven years (Daniel 9:27). But in the middle of that "seven" he will put an end to Israel's sacrifices and will set up an abomination. These statements are picked up by Jesus in the New Testament as references to the Antichrist's intrusion into the Temple and the setting up of an image of himself to be worshiped (Matthew 24:15 – 21).

Daniel's framework of seven years also fits the time references in the book of Revelation. Various phrases mark out the two halves of the Tribulation as three and a half years each.

- Revelation 11:2

  "42 months" — the time the Gentiles will trample on the city of Jerusalem and defile the Temple; the second half of the Tribulation

- Revelation 11:3

  "1,260 days" — the period of time that two witnesses sent from God will prophesy before the Antichrist kills them at the middle point of the Tribulation; the first half of the Tribulation

- Revelation 12:6

  "1,260 days" — the woman [Israel] flees from Satan's persecution and is protected in the desert of Judea; the second half of the Tribulation

- Revelation 12:14

  "a time, times and half a time" — another reference to the time Israel will flee from Satan's persecution and be protected by God in the desert; I take the phrase to mean "a year, two years and a half a year," or three and a half years; the second half of the Tribulation

- Revelation 13:5

  "forty-two months" — the period of time the beast is given power to continue his oppression; the second half of the Tribulation

The time references in Revelation fit precisely with Daniel's prediction of a final seven-year period of distress for Israel.

So when you hear a prophecy preacher refer to "Daniel's seventieth week," you will know that he's talking about the future seven years of the Tribulation. The first sixty-nine "weeks" of years are already ancient history; the final "week" of years is yet to come.

HELP FILE

HISTORY BEFORE IT HAPPENS

A Futurist's View of the Tribulation

I am persuaded that the Tribulation is still future. It will be a time of God's judgment on a world that has rejected him. Here's how events of the Tribulation will unfold. Not all futurists agree with every detail, but this seems to be the most consistent view of how things will go. God has given us a lot of detailed information about those crucial seven years — and they are still to come!

First Three and a Half Years

The Tribulation will begin when a powerful political leader makes a treaty with the nation of Israel. The treaty will guarantee Israel's political safety or (perhaps) will grant Israel the right to begin to offer sacrifices to God in a rebuilt or reclaimed Temple in Jerusalem. *Daniel 9:27; in Revelation 11:1 – 2, a rebuilt Temple is pictured*

In his vision of heaven, the apostle John sees Jesus (the Lamb) take a scroll from God the Father and begin to break the seven wax seals on the scroll. As each seal is broken, a new judgment sweeps over the earth. *Revelation 5 – 7*

- The first seal: A conqueror on a white horse (Revelation 6:1 – 2) — the emergence of the Antichrist on the world scene as a persuasive leader

- The second seal: A rider on a red horse (Revelation 6:3 – 4) — wars and threats of wars shake human society

- The third seal: A rider on a black horse (Revelation 6:5 – 6) — wars and upheaval produce famine in some parts of the world

- The fourth seal: A rider on a pale horse (Revelation 6:7 – 8) — death claims one-fourth of the earth's population

- The fifth seal: Men and women killed because of their loyalty to Jesus cry out for God's judgment on the world (Revelation 6:9 – 11)

- The sixth seal: A great earthquake and cosmic disturbances (Revelation 6:12 – 17)

- The seventh seal: Silence in heaven as seven angels with trumpets prepare to unleash the next wave of judgments on the earth (Revelation 8:1 – 2)

The seal judgments are dreadful but not as severe as later judgments. Each of these catastrophes can be attributed to purely human initiative or to natural disasters. Later judgments are clearly the intervention of God.

The Four Horsemen

The first four seal judgments are pictured as riders on (different) colored horses. These four riders are called "the four horsemen of the Apocalypse" and are often used in literature or art as symbols of doom or of the end of the world.

Techno-Speak

The political leader who made the treaty with Israel will gradually gain more power. Some of this power he will gain through military conquest; some will come through diplomatic pressure. In time he will head a confederation of ten western nations, centered in the old Roman Empire. *Daniel pictured this ten-nation confederation emerging from the historical and cultural remnants of Rome (Daniel 2:40 – 43; 7:23 – 25; see also Revelation 13:1; 17:12, 16).*

In Israel, God will raise up two witnesses to speak a message of warning to the people. These two witnesses will be like Old Testament prophets with power to confirm the truth of their message with miracles. Through their testimony, 144,000 Jews will believe in Jesus and will be sealed with God's protection. *Revelation 7:1 – 8; 11:1 – 14*

The 144,000 Messianic Jews (as in, Jews who believe in Jesus as the true Messiah) will be scattered throughout the world to preach the message of Jesus' soon return to earth in visible glory. Thousands of people will receive their message! One of the greatest revivals to sweep the world will take place during the Tribulation. Many of those who believe in Jesus, however, will be killed by the Antichrist because of their allegiance to Jesus. *Revelation 7:9 – 17*

The Middle of the Tribulation

At the midpoint of the seven years of distress, seven trumpet judgments will fall on humankind. Seven angels in heaven blow seven trumpets, and each trumpet blast unleashes a new catastrophe on earth.

- The first trumpet: Hail and fire fall on the earth; one-third of the vegetation is destroyed (Revelation 8:6 – 7)
- The second trumpet: A huge burning mountain is thrown into the sea; one-third of all sea life dies (Revelation 8:8 – 9)
- The third trumpet: A great star (meteor?) falls from heaven and pollutes the freshwater sources; many people die from the poisoned water (Revelation 8:10 – 11)
- The fourth trumpet: The sun, moon, and stars are diminished by one-third (Revelation 8:12 – 13)
- The fifth trumpet: An angel opens a stronghold where demonic forces have been confined; these locustlike beings swarm out to torment humankind for five months (Revelation 9:1 – 12)
- The sixth trumpet: Massive armies from the east begin to move toward Israel, spreading destruction in their path (Revelation 9:13 – 21)

THE TWO WITNESSES

As the visions of the book of Revelation unfold, John hears about two witnesses who will speak with God's authority for "1,260 days" (about three and a half years). These two witnesses are given certain powers that remind us of the powers given to some Old Testament prophets.

- "If anyone tries to harm them, fire comes from their mouths and devours their enemies" (Revelation 11:5).

In the Old Testament book of 2 Kings, we are told that King Ahaziah sent soldiers to arrest the prophet Elijah, and fire came down from heaven and consumed the soldiers (2 Kings 1:10, 12).

- "These men have power to shut up the sky so that it will not rain" (Revelation 11:6).

Sounds like Elijah again, who asked God to stop the rain as a judgment on the idol-worshiping nation of Israel (1 Kings 17:1). It didn't rain for three and a half years — just like the future Tribulation rainless period (Luke 4:25; James 5:17).

- "They have power to turn the waters into blood and to strike the earth with every kind of plague as often as they want" (Revelation 11:6).

This verse reminds us of the prophet Moses, who brought plagues on Egypt when the pharaoh refused to release the people of Israel from slavery (Exodus 7:17 – 21; also Exodus 8 – 11).

Because these two guys sound so much like Elijah and Moses, some people think that God will bring these same two prophets back to earth as his witnesses during the Tribulation. Others have proposed Elijah and Enoch as likely candidates. Enoch lived long before Israel's great father, Abraham. Enoch was taken directly to heaven without dying (Genesis 5:24; Hebrews 11:5). The prophet Elijah left planet Earth in the same way — in a fiery chariot that took him directly to heaven (2 Kings 2:11 – 12). Since these two men did not die (so the argument goes), they may be the ones who return to earth as God's witnesses and suffer death in the Tribulation.

The Bible doesn't directly support any of these identifications. I think it's safest to say that these two witnesses have powers *similar* to the powers of Elijah and Moses, but they will probably be two new prophets sent from God.

The two witnesses preach in Israel during the first three and a half years of the Tribulation. When the Antichrist invades Israel, however, one of his first priorities is to get rid of the witnesses. They are killed, and their bodies lie in the streets of Jerusalem for three and a half days. But then they are raised back to life and taken into heaven in a cloud. If that isn't enough to shake up the Antichrist, God sends a powerful earthquake through the city that destroys a tenth of the buildings. Seven thousand people die in the aftermath. *(Read the account yourself in Revelation 11:7 – 13.)*

THE 144,000

The Bible's image of 144,000 dedicated servants of God has stirred controversy and debate for nearly two thousand years. Everyone wants to be part of that group!

Charles Russell (1852 – 1916), one of the founders of the movement called the Jehovah's Witnesses, claimed that God was choosing a church out of the world, to be made up of 144,000 "spiritual Israelites." These kings-priests would reign with Christ in the thousand-year Kingdom on earth. When Russell's followers numbered *more* than 144,000, Russell added a second class of heavenly servants — the "great company" or "other sheep."

Some Christians believe that the number is symbolic for all those who remain faithful to Christ during times of persecution. Other Christians believe that John's words are to be taken more literally. They believe that the 144,000 are Jews (note that the twelve tribes or clans of Israel are listed in Revelation) who will spread the message of Christ throughout the world during the Tribulation.

The only two passages in the Bible that refer to the 144,000 are Revelation 7:1 – 8 and 14:1 – 5.

- The seventh trumpet: Those in heaven rejoice over God's ultimate triumph (Revelation 11:15 – 19)

On earth, the Antichrist invades Israel and kills God's two witnesses, who are raised back to life after three and a half days and taken into heaven in a cloud. *Revelation 11:1 – 13*

Satan is thrown out of heaven and confined to the earth. Today Satan has access into God's presence, but at that point he will be excluded from heaven's realm. Satan is enraged as he sees God's plan moving perfectly toward final victory. *Revelation 12:7 – 12*

The Antichrist suffers what seems to be a fatal wound to his head (perhaps an assassination) but miraculously survives. To people who are aware of God's Word, the Antichrist is exposed as the instrument of Satan's power. Unbelieving people stand in awe of the Antichrist. *Revelation 13:1 – 10*

The Antichrist enters the rebuilt Temple in Jerusalem and proclaims himself to be a god. Another leader, the false prophet, comes on the scene to direct the religious worship of the Antichrist. He sets up an image of the Antichrist in the Temple and demands that the world worship the image. *2 Thessalonians 2:3 – 4, 8 – 10; Revelation 11:1 – 2; 13:11 – 15*

The Jews recognize their betrayal by the Antichrist and run away from his persecution. God protects some of the Jews in the Judean desert. *Revelation 12:6, 13 – 17; Matthew 24:15 – 22*

The false prophet requires every person in the Antichrist's realm to be branded or tattooed with a mark of allegiance to the Antichrist. Without the mark on their forehead or right hand, no one can buy, sell, hold a job, or avoid arrest. *Revelation 13:16 – 18*

The Final Three and a Half Years

In heaven, seven angels appear, carrying bowls that represent God's wrath. As each bowl is poured out, new catastrophes blast the earth.

Points 2 Remember

☑ Christians who believe that the Tribulation is still future see it as a seven-year period of drastic judgment from God.

☑ Satan will be active during the Tribulation. He will empower an evil world ruler (the Antichrist) and his religious cult leader (the false prophet).

☑ The Antichrist will declare himself to be a god and will pursue world domination. His identifying mark (the "mark of the beast") will be required for any commercial activity.

☑ The Tribulation will end in the battle of Armageddon and the return of Jesus to earth in visible glory.

- The first bowl: Painful sores fall on all those who have the Antichrist's mark (Revelation 16:2)
- The second bowl: The oceans turn to blood and all sea life dies (Revelation 16:3)
- The third bowl: Fresh water turns to blood (Revelation 16:4 – 7)
- The fourth bowl: The sun scorches human beings with intense heat (Revelation 16:8 – 9)
- The fifth bowl: Agonizing darkness falls over the Antichrist's realm (Revelation 16:10 – 11)
- The sixth bowl: The Euphrates River dries up to prepare the way for armies from the east (Revelation 16:12)
- The seventh bowl: A devastating earthquake rocks the earth, and huge hailstones fall from the sky (Revelation 16:17 – 21)

On earth, the Antichrist gathers his military forces in Israel to meet the armies coming from the east in a final battle, the battle of Armageddon. *Revelation 16:13 – 16; Daniel 11:40 – 45*

The Antichrist either defeats the eastern army or persuades them to join him against the Jews still living in Israel. The Antichrist seeks to destroy the people of Israel once and for all. The Jews turn in repentance to God, and Jesus returns from heaven in majesty and power. Jesus crushes the vast armies of the Antichrist and throws the Antichrist and the false prophet into the lake of fire. *Revelation 19:11 – 21; Zechariah 12:2 – 5, 8 – 10; Matthew 24:29 – 30*

Those human beings still alive on earth after the battle of Armageddon are judged by Jesus. The Jews are regathered to Israel by God's angels for judgment. Those who have believed in Jesus as their Messiah enter the Kingdom that Jesus establishes on earth. Those who have not believed die. *Matthew 24:31; Ezekiel 20:33 – 44*

Non-Jews (Gentiles) are also judged. Angels sweep over the earth and remove through death all those who have not believed in Jesus and who have received the Antichrist's mark. Anyone who has believed in Jesus and remained faithful to him will be ushered into the abundance of Jesus' earthly Kingdom. *Matthew 13:40 – 43; 24:36 – 44; 25:31 – 46*

DiGGinG DeEpeR

In addition to the resources listed on page 60, you might want to read the popular fictionalized account of what life will be like during the Tribulation found in the Left Behind series of novels by Tim LaHaye and Jerry Jenkins. Not everyone agrees with the picture painted in these books. Take a look, for example, at Gary DeMar's book, *End Times Fiction: A Biblical Consideration of the Left Behind Theology* (Nashville: Nelson, 2001). DeMar holds to the view that the predictions about the Tribulation were fulfilled when Rome destroyed Jerusalem in A.D. 70.

CHAPTER 4

Enter the Beast:
The Antichrist

Enter the Beast: The Antichrist

Heads Up

▸ Meet the "Future Führer" — the evil world ruler called the Antichrist

▸ Find out what Napoleon, Ronald Reagan, and Saddam Hussein have in common

▸ "666" on your license plate — coincidence or a sign of Satan?

We've seen some pretty nasty leaders come and go in the last two thousand years. Men and women who rise to power and leave a legacy of oppression, war, and murder. Joseph Stalin, Adolf Hitler, Pol Pot, and Idi Amin were among the worst of the last century — and others are poised to inhabit the moral sewers of the next century.

As incredibly evil as these lowlifes of the past have been, the worst is yet to come. The Bible predicts the rise of a future ruler who will set out to conquer the world — and who will almost succeed. He will demand not simply loyalty from his subjects but worship. Those who resist or refuse will be crushed. This future ruler is called the beast, or the Antichrist.

Bible Networking

Antichrist

Most of what we know about the Antichrist comes from three essential go-to sections of the Bible:

- Daniel 11:36 – 12:1
- 2 Thessalonians 2:1 – 10
- Revelation 13:1 – 9

Future or Past?

Some Christians do not think that the Antichrist will rise up in the future because they are convinced he made his appearance in the past. Most of our information about the Antichrist comes from the New Testament book of Revelation — the last book in the Bible. Revelation is the record of a series of visions that God gave to an early Christian leader, the apostle John. John was under arrest when he wrote the book — exiled to the prison island of Patmos. It was a time of intense persecution of Christians, and John, as one of the most prominent Christian leaders, was sentenced to separation from other Christians.

Some interpreters of Revelation believe that as John wrote the book he was writing about his own time, not a future time. John was producing a sketch of events going on around him, but in a prophetic "code" that only other Christians would understand. According to this view, when John saw "a beast coming out of the sea" (13:1) who demanded the worship of the world, John was not describing some future world ruler but the "beastly" Roman emperor of his own day. One of the issues that got early Christians into trouble was their refusal to offer an

Techno-Speak

Four Views

The view that the book of Revelation is a veiled protest against the evil of the first-century Roman Empire is called the *preterist* view. According to this approach, John saw the Roman Empire as a horrible beast bent on crushing the Christian church. John wrote down his visions as an encouragement to Christians undergoing persecution.

A related interpretive approach is the *historicist* view. Those who interpret Revelation from this perspective see the book as a continuous description of the events in history from John's day through the present day and up to the return of Jesus from heaven. The problem for these folks is to figure out which world events fit the events John describes in his visions. According to one scholar who holds this view, the beast in Revelation 13 is the Roman Catholic Church and the popes who have led it.

The view I embrace for interpreting Revelation is called the *futurist* view. This view holds that all of John's visions from Revelation 4:1 through the end of the book are yet to be fulfilled. John is clearly told in Revelation 4:1 that he would be shown events that "must take place *after this*," that is, after John's own lifetime. According to this approach, the beast is a still future world ruler who rises to great power during the Tribulation.

A fourth major interpretive approach is called the *idealist* view. According to this view, Revelation describes the eternal conflict between good and evil throughout every age. The events John describes do not correspond to historical events past or present but dramatize the struggle between a rebellious creation and a God who is steadily bringing everything back under his authority. The beast in chapter 13, according to this view, represents state authority that rises up in persecution of the church. Such "Antichrists" have appeared several times in history.

annual tribute to the Roman emperor. Every citizen was required to go down to city hall, offer a pinch of incense on an altar to the emperor, and say publicly, "Caesar is Lord!" This was no big deal for most of the pagan people of the empire, but Christians acknowledged only *one* Lord — Jesus Christ. Believe it or not, the Christians were charged with *atheism* (a belief in no gods — at least no visible gods). They were also charged with treason because they acknowledged a ruler higher than the emperor. For those "crimes" Christians were killed in the arenas, crucified, and burned alive.

The apostle John's visions conclude with Jesus returning from heaven in great power to destroy the beast and to rescue Christians from a collapsing world. This didn't happen in John's day, of course, but those who interpret Revelation in a purely historical framework believe that this is what John *hoped* would happen. It expressed his hope that Jesus would return and conquer evil forever.

This "happened in the past" approach to understanding Revelation has some interesting features — and there are some definite parallels between what John wrote and what was happening in John's world — but it ignores the clear future focus of John's visions. The book itself claims to be a "prophecy" (1:3), or vision of the future. Jesus told John that he would show him things that would happen *after* the events of his own day. John's prediction of Jesus' return from heaven to destroy evil and to set up his own Kingdom of good was not just a hopeful wish of John's but a clear promise of events still to happen. Furthermore, other writers in the Bible talk about the Antichrist and (like John) portray the Antichrist as a *future* world leader. Evil Roman emperors and even wicked modern leaders may bear some resemblance to the Antichrist, but only one evil "beast" will fulfill the Bible's predictions completely.

Person or Power?

Some Christians view the beast of Revelation as a symbol of evil and of oppressive governments. They see the book of Revelation as a parable of God's ultimate triumph over evil and over a world marked by rebellion against him. The beast (according to this view) is not a literal person in the past or in the future but the embodiment of humanity's

A BLAST FROM THE PAST

The Old Testament prophet Daniel wrote his book almost six hundred years before Jesus was born. In his book Daniel accurately predicted the rise of an evil king four hundred years later who would oppress Israel and desecrate God's Temple in Jerusalem.

Antiochus Epiphanes (an-**tie**-o-cuss ee-**pi**-fan-ees) was a Greek-speaking king who ruled over Syria (north of the land of Israel) between 175 and 163 B.C. Antiochus invaded Israel in 168 B.C. and did his best to eradicate the worship of the Lord God. He told the Jews that they could not worship on the Sabbath. He prohibited circumcision, the observance of religious festivals, and the offering of animal sacrifices in the Temple. Copies of the Hebrew Bible were to be burned, and Jews were ordered to eat pork (a meat prohibited by God's Law).

In what was the worst crime of all in the eyes of the Jews, Antiochus ordered that a pig (a ceremonially unclean animal) was to be offered as a sacrifice in God's Temple. The sacrifice was to be dedicated to Zeus and to the new god-king, Antiochus himself. A Jewish revolt, led by Judas Maccabeus, eventually drove Antiochus and his army out of Palestine. The Temple was cleansed and the worship of God was restored — an event Jewish people still celebrate each year at Hanukkah.

Daniel saw more in Antiochus than just an evil ruler. Antiochus was a foreshadowing of the future Antichrist. Both men would proclaim themselves to be gods; both would invade Israel; both would turn against Jews who refused their new worship program; both would desecrate the Temple in Jerusalem — and both would ultimately be destroyed.

For more on Antiochus Epiphanes, read Daniel 8:8 – 27; 11:29 – 35 and in the Apocrypha, 1 Maccabees 1 – 6.

sinful uprising against God in every age. Ultimately God's grace and God's power will conquer human sin and restore humanity to God's ideal society.

Those who take a purely symbolic view of the beast point to some passages in the Bible where the term "antichrist" does not mean an individual person but a willful spirit of disobedience to God.

> Dear children, this is the last hour; and as you have heard that the antichrist is coming, even now many antichrists have come. This is how we know it is the last hour. (1 John 2:18)

> Who is the liar? It is the man who denies that Jesus is the Christ. Such a man is the antichrist — he denies the Father and the Son. (1 John 2:22)

Every spirit that does not acknowledge Jesus is not from God. This is the spirit of the antichrist, which you have heard is coming and even now is already in the world. (1 John 4:3)

Many deceivers, who do not acknowledge Jesus Christ as coming in the flesh, have gone out into the world. Any such person is the deceiver and the antichrist. (2 John 7)

All these passages were written by the apostle John — the same man who wrote the book of Revelation and who talked about "the beast."

A FEW VIEWS ON THE BEAST

Quotation Marks

"Who is the beast of John's vision? . . . There is little doubt that for John the beast was the Roman Empire as persecutor of the church. . . . Yet the beast is more than the Roman Empire. . . . The beast has always been the deification of secular authority."

Robert Mounce, in *The Book of Revelation,* New International Commentary on the New Testament (Grand Rapids: Eerdmans, 1977), 251

"Nero is at least a prima facie candidate for the role of the beast. As described by ancient historians, Nero is a singularly cruel and unrestrained man of evil."

R. C. Sproul, in *The Last Days according to Jesus* (Grand Rapids: Baker, 1998), 186 – 87

"The Antichrist is presented in Scripture as a literal person who will be revealed to this world scene immediately after the rapture of the church. . . . There [have been] many partial manifestations of the Antichrist during the course of world history which will lead up to his final revelation during the last days."

Walter K. Price, in *The Coming Antichrist* (Chicago: Moody Press, 1974), 12, 17

"For you ought to know and to believe, and hold it for certain, that the day of affliction has begun to hang over our heads, and the end of the world and the time of Antichrist [have begun] to draw near, so that we must all stand prepared for the battle."

Cyprian (A.D. 200 – 258), Bishop of Carthage, in *Epistle 55*

BEASTLY NAMES

The Bible uses several names and titles to describe the future Antichrist. I've listed them in the reverse order in which they appear in the Bible because the later names are the clearest.

Revelation 13:1	The Beast
1 John 2:18	The Antichrist
2 Thessalonians 2:8	The Lawless One
2 Thessalonians 2:3	The Man Doomed to Destruction
2 Thessalonians 2:3	The Man of Lawlessness
Zechariah 11:15 – 17	The Foolish Shepherd/The Worthless Shepherd
Daniel 11:36	The King
Daniel 11:21	A Contemptible Person
Daniel 9:26	The Ruler Who Will Come
Daniel 7:8	A Little Horn

(Interestingly, John never uses the word *antichrist* in the book of Revelation.) In the verses above, it sounds as though the antichrist is not some future ruler but a present, pervading spirit in human culture. At the same time, John is not denying the appearance of a future evil ruler. He says, in fact, that "the antichrist *is* coming" (1 John 2:18, emphasis added). The evil tendencies that will find fulfillment in the future Antichrist are already alive and active in our world today. The *spirit* of opposition to God is already at work; the *fulfillment* of that spirit will be accomplished in one person who rises to world power and sets himself against God.

What John Saw

As the visions of Revelation unfolded, God gave the apostle John a stunning picture of the Antichrist:

> And I saw a beast coming out of the sea. He had ten horns and seven heads, with ten crowns on his horns, and on each head a blasphemous name. The beast I saw resembled a leopard, but had feet like those of a bear and a mouth like that of a lion. The dragon gave the beast his power and his throne and great authority. (Revelation 13:1 – 2)

John was not reading words in a book as he wrote this. He actually *saw* this happening in a vision. He saw images that represented aspects of the Antichrist's character and power.

The beast, for example, had ten horns and seven heads. This doesn't mean that the Antichrist will literally have seven heads. Later in Revelation John is told what the horns and heads represent. The seven heads are seven kings (Revelation 17:9 – 10). The prophet Daniel had already predicted that the Antichrist would control a ten-nation confederation but would personally rule three nations, leaving seven other nations that he would control indirectly (Daniel 7:24 – 25). The ten horns also represent kings (Revelation 17:12 – 14). They rule independently only for a short time and then give their authority to the beast.

The beast looked to John like a leopard (swift, deadly) but also had some features like a bear (powerful) and a lion (terrifying). Again, the Antichrist will not literally have animal features, but the symbol represents aspects of his character as well as his effect on people around him. The Old Testament prophet Daniel had used the same animals to picture the "beastly" nature of other world empires, empires that existed long ago. The future beast will combine the worst of the old and the worst of the new.

Who Is Like the Beast? The Character of the Antichrist

You might get the idea from hearing him called "the beast" that the Antichrist will be a raving, frothing-at-the-mouth lunatic! But that's not the case. *God* calls him the beast because this term accurately describes his true character, while the world will hail the Antichrist as a great leader, a savior.

2 Thessalonians 2:8

And then the lawless one will be revealed, whom the Lord Jesus will overthrow with the breath of his mouth and destroy by the splendor of his coming.

The word *antichrist* means a substitute Christ, a person who is totally the opposite of the true Christ and totally opposed to the true Christ. The beast will come on the scene as an acclaimed hero — a deliverer (a substitute Christ) — but his goal will be oppression and personal power (the exact opposite of Jesus' goals). In many respects the Antichrist will be the most remarkable political figure the world has ever seen. He will be easy to like and even easier to follow.

Let me give you the list of his character qualities from his biblical résumé:

- *He will be wiser and more powerful than any other political leader in history.* People the world over will say, "Who is like the beast? Who can make war against him?" (Revelation 13:4).
- *He will be a persuasive speaker and a cunning politician.* When he speaks, nations will be swayed by his words (Daniel 7:8; Revelation 13:5). He will even persuade the majority to worship him (Revelation 13:8).
- *His political power and military strength will cause the whole world to stand in awe* (Revelation 13:3; 17:8). The Antichrist will succeed by war and by peace! He will give the impression that he has the answer to world peace by appearing to resolve several long-standing disputes, particularly in the Middle East.

But as appealing as the Antichrist will seem on television and in the media reports of his accomplishments, he will have the inner character of a wild animal. He will embody pride, arrogance, and ambition like no one else ever has.

- *He will worship power.* Daniel says that "he will honor a god of fortresses" (Daniel 11:38). He will claim to be the most highly evolved being on the planet, worthy of the trust and obedience of everyone.
- *He will hate God.* The Antichrist will not be an atheist! He will admit that God exists, but he will hate God. His words will be venomous attacks on the character of God. "He will exalt and magnify himself above every god and will say unheard-of things against the God of gods" (Daniel 11:36). The Antichrist will even proclaim himself to be the one god worthy of the world's worship (2 Thessalonians 2:4).

"AND THE NOMINEES ARE . . ."

Since the early years of the church, Christians have fingered a wide variety of people as the Antichrist. Some believe that Judas Iscariot, the disciple who betrayed Jesus, would be revived from the dead and become the Antichrist. (This view is based on the fact that both Judas and the Antichrist are called "the son of perdition" in the King James Version of the Bible; see John 17:12 and 2 Thessalonians 2:3.) Other Christians in the early centuries of the church were convinced that the Roman emperor Nero would return from the dead (or had never really died) and would come back as the Antichrist.

In every age Christians have continued to speculate. Michael Holmes on page 241 in his *NIV Application Commentary* on 1 and 2 Thessalonians (Grand Rapids: Zondervan, 1998) gives an incredible list of people who have been identified at one time or another as the Antichrist:

Various Roman emperors	King Faisal of Saudi Arabia
Muhammad	The United Nations
Various popes and the papacy itself	Khruschev
Emperor Frederick II and Pope Gregory IX (each of whom proclaimed the other as the Antichrist)	The old Soviet Union
Martin Luther	Mikhail Gorbachev (the birthmark on his forehead was alleged to be the mark of the beast)
King George II of England	Pope John Paul II
Napoleon	Anwar Sadat
Each side in the American Civil War	The Ayatollah Khomeini
Kaiser Wilhelm of Germany	Yasser Arafat
The League of Nations	Saddam Hussein
Hitler	Henry Kissinger
Mussolini	President Jimmy Carter
Stalin	

And the list still goes on! Just go to any Christian bookstore and look at the *Prophecy* section. *Someone* will have a book claiming that they've figured out who the Antichrist really is.

Hint: Remember this list, and don't buy the book!!

BARNEY AND THE BEAST

This humorous "Antichrist Alert" made its way around the Internet a while ago — the "proof" that the cute purple dinosaur Barney is really the beast in disguise!

1. Start with his standard description:
   CUTE PURPLE DINOSAUR

2. Change all U's to V's (which is proper Latin anyway):
   CVTE PVRPLE DINOSAVR

3. Extract all Roman numerals in the phrase:
   C / V / V / L / D / I / V

4. Convert the value of the Roman numerals to Arabic numbers:
   100 / 5 / 5 / 50 / 500 / 1 / 5

5. Add all the numbers:
   666

Barney Is the Beast!!

- *He will refuse to submit to any law but his own.* Simply put, the Antichrist will "do as he pleases" (Daniel 11:36). The apostle Paul calls him "the lawless one" (2 Thessalonians 2:8). The spirit of lawlessness and rebellion already permeates our society, but that spirit is held in check by God's Holy Spirit. When God removes the Spirit's restraining power, humanity's bent toward anarchy and lawlessness will be virtually unhindered (2 Thessalonians 2:7). The only rebellion the Antichrist will not tolerate is rebellion against his own rule and authority. Those who dare to defy him will be crushed.
- *He will be the epitome of selfish ambition.* The Antichrist will appear humble and compassionate for a while, but ultimately he will exalt and magnify himself (Daniel 11:36 – 37; 2 Thessalonians 2:4). His self-exalting attitude is the very heart of what it means to sin against God.

A Spectacular Rise: The Antichrist's Career — Phase One

The Antichrist's career stretches over the full seven years of the future Tribulation period. (See chapter 3 for a discussion of the Tribulation.) The first three and a half years are fairly calm, but then a crisis launches the Antichrist to a whole new level of power.

Here's how events will unfold. Not every student of biblical prophecy will agree with every point in the order I've listed them, but things will generally go like this:

Politically, the Antichrist will begin his career as a fairly inconspicuous person. He will probably be in a position of some political power when the Tribulation begins (although we've seen some individuals rise rather quickly from relative obscurity to great power). Because Daniel sees the Antichrist first appear as "a little horn," it seems that the Antichrist will start out as a minor player on the political stage.

At the precise moment in God's plan, however, the Antichrist will begin to extend his power rapidly. Daniel predicted that the Antichrist would gain power within the context of the old Roman Empire. Some Bible teachers believe the Antichrist will rule over Europe (the area of the original Roman Empire). I'm inclined to believe that the Antichrist will rise to power in a western nation (Europe or North America) and eventually will dominate the western world — the part of the world that has basic cultural links to the Roman Empire.

Within a short period of time, the Antichrist consolidates his political and military control over a ten-nation confederation. He may conquer some of these nations militarily, but, more likely, he will be given control because of his ability to resolve conflicts and govern with such skill.

The world will be in a state of political turmoil when the Antichrist comes on the scene. Wars and threatened wars will add to the confusion. As judgments from God begin to sweep over the world in the early part of the Tribulation, one-fourth of the world's population will die (Revelation 6:8). Conditions will be right for the rise of a strong ruler. Desperate people will follow him without question. The Bible also makes it clear that God will allow the vast majority of people living on earth to be deluded by this evil ruler. They will believe his lies (2 Thessalonians 2:11).

The Antichrist will control a powerful, multination confederation. He will set up a political dictatorship based on overwhelming military power. At first the people under his authority will welcome his strong-handed control, but over time his rule will become more and more oppressive.

A REBUILT TEMPLE?

The New Testament says that the Antichrist ("the man of lawlessness") will enter the Temple and declare himself to be god (2 Thessalonians 2:4). Only one problem — there is no Temple in Jerusalem today! On the basis of that prophecy, many Christians believe that the Temple in Jerusalem will be rebuilt — perhaps during the first half of the Tribulation or even before the Tribulation begins.

A look at Israel's Temple in the past will give us some perspective on the future:

- When Moses received the Law (the Ten Commandments and the regulations for Old Testament worship) from God, he also received instructions for constructing a portable worship center for Israel. The tentlike structure, surrounded by a screened-in courtyard, was called the *tabernacle*. Whenever the people of Israel set out, the tabernacle was disassembled and moved with them. Once the people of Israel settled in the land of Canaan, the tabernacle was set up at Shiloh. The people came to the tabernacle to offer the animal sacrifices required by the Law.

- Later in Israel's history, King David wanted to build a permanent place of worship in Jerusalem. God did not allow David to build it, but God did command David's son, Solomon, to pursue his father's dream. The spot chosen by God was Mount Moriah in Jerusalem — the place where Abraham offered his son, Isaac, as a sacrifice to God and where God provided a ram to die in place of Isaac (Genesis 22:2; 1 Chronicles 21:18 – 22:1; 2 Chronicles 3:1). The *first Temple* was finished in 960 B.C. It was a magnificent structure dedicated to the Lord. The first Temple was destroyed by the Babylonian army in 586 B.C. — it had stood for 374 years.

- The *second Temple* was begun after some of the Jews returned from captivity in Babylon in 536 B.C. It was finished in 515 B.C. but was much smaller and far less glorious than Solomon's Temple. Almost 500 years later, Herod the Great, in order to win favor with the Jews, began a massive expansion and beautification of the Temple in 20 B.C. The work was finally finished in A.D. 63. Herod's Temple was the building Jesus knew. The second Temple was destroyed in A.D. 70 by the Roman armies — it had lasted for 586 years.

- Since A.D. 70 the Jewish people have not had a temple in which sacrifices could be offered to God.

- In A.D. 638, just six years after the death of Muhammad, Muslim armies conquered Palestine under Caliph Omar. Muslims believe that Mount Moriah was the place from which Muhammad was taken to heaven in a vision. In order to honor this sacred spot, the Mosque of Omar was built over Mount Moriah in

continued at top of next page

A.D. 691. The complex is known today as the Dome of the Rock and has covered that site for more than 1300 years.

- Here's the problem with rebuilding Israel's Temple (a third Temple): How can Israel build a temple on the same spot occupied by a Muslim mosque? Perhaps a compromise will be worked out, or maybe the Antichrist will give Israel authority to occupy the site, but it seems likely that a *Tribulational Temple* will be built. It is this Temple that the Antichrist will use as the center of the world's worship during the last half of the Tribulation.

- A fourth Temple will be built in Jerusalem during the future thousand-year reign of Jesus on earth. This *Millennial Temple* is described in great detail in Ezekiel 40 – 48. Animal sacrifices will be offered during the Kingdom — not to take away sin (that was accomplished forever by Jesus on the cross), but as a memorial to Jesus' final sacrifice.

In his new position of power, the Antichrist makes a treaty with the nation of Israel and guarantees Israel's security in the Middle East (Daniel 9:27). The Antichrist appears to solve the long-standing problems between Israel and her Arab neighbors. Israel proclaims the arrival of peace. The people of Israel even begin to rebuild their Temple, the center of worship to the Lord.

As the middle of the Tribulation approaches, the Antichrist will have consolidated his power over the western world and become Israel's protector. But events at the three-and-a-half-year mark of the Tribulation push the Antichrist to a new level of ruthless oppression.

The Mark of the Beast: The Antichrist's Career — Phase Two

Near the midpoint of the seven-year Tribulation, powerful nations decide to invade Israel. The Antichrist uses this threatened invasion as an opportunity to enter Israel himself. He defeats the opposing armies (called, in Daniel 11:40 – 43, the king of the North and the king of the South) and conquers the entire region of southwest Asia and north Africa, the area we call the Middle East.

In the course of the conquest, the Antichrist is fatally wounded. I think this will be an actual physical wound in the head, perhaps from an assassin's hand or a military attack. (Some interpreters think it is a political "wound" — a challenge to the Antichrist's supremacy, which he is able to survive.) The Antichrist dies or comes close to death, but Satan, the enemy of God, intervenes and miraculously raises the Antichrist back to life.

In Revelation 13, as John describes his vision of the Antichrist, he writes, "One of the heads of the beast seemed to have had a fatal wound, but the fatal wound had been healed. The whole world was astonished and followed the beast" (Revelation 13:3). Later John describes the Antichrist as the one "whose fatal wound had been healed" (13:12) and the one "who was wounded by the sword and yet lived" (13:14).

As the world stands amazed at his miraculous recovery, the Antichrist uses the opportunity to begin his final plan for world domination. He enters the Jewish temple in Jerusalem and proclaims himself to be a god!

> He will oppose and will exalt himself over everything that is called God or is worshiped, so that he sets himself up in God's temple, proclaiming himself to be God. (2 Thessalonians 2:4)

JEW OR GENTILE? MALE OR FEMALE?

Students of prophecy are divided over whether the Antichrist will be a Jew or a non-Jew (Gentile). Those who think the Antichrist will be a Jew base their conclusion on the assumption that the Jews will accept the Antichrist (for a while) as their promised Messiah.

But while the Antichrist will ensure Israel's political and military security, there is no indication that he will be regarded as the Messiah promised by God in the Old Testament. He will be a political deliverer in a sense, but he will not restore a glorious Kingdom to Israel (as God said the Messiah would). Furthermore, the beast in Revelation 13:1 is said to come "out of the sea." The sea is used frequently in prophetic visions to picture the nations of the world (Isaiah 57:20; Luke 21:25 – 26; Revelation 17:15). The Antichrist *does* come on the world scene as a substitute Christ — but in *opposition* to the true Christ. He could be of Jewish origin, but more likely (in my opinion, at least) he will be a Gentile.

The evidence is more conclusive for the gender of the Antichrist. Daniel, Paul, and John all repeatedly refer to the Antichrist as a male. They refer to him always as "he," not "she" or "it."

HELP FiLe
NO LIMITS

The apostle Paul let the Christians in the city of Thessalonica in on some secret information about the Antichrist:

> Don't you remember that when I was with you I used to tell you these things? And now you know what is holding [the Antichrist] back, so that he may be revealed at the proper time. For the secret power of lawlessness is already at work; but the one who now holds it back will continue to do so till he is taken out of the way. And then the lawless one will be revealed, whom the Lord Jesus will overthrow with the breath of his mouth and destroy by the splendor of his coming.

> 2 Thessalonians 2:5 – 8

The *power* of lawlessness was already at work in the first century to oppose God, but someone or something was holding back the full expression of humanity's evil. The *person* of lawlessness will not be revealed until after the restraining power is taken out of the way. So who is holding evil back, and when will that restraint be removed?

Three suggestions for the restrainer:

The Holy Spirit. Right now the Holy Spirit (God the Spirit, the third person of the Trinity) is active in our world to restrain and control evil. At some point in the future, the Spirit will take his hands off, and Satan will be allowed to bring his evil masterpiece, the Antichrist, onto the world stage.

Christians/the Church. Some interpreters believe that the presence of true Christians has a preserving and restraining effect on the world. When true Christians are removed from the earth in the rapture (assuming you believe that the rapture will come *before* the Tribulation begins), the restraints on human sin will also be removed and the Antichrist will make his appearance.

Civil Government. Other interpreters think that the restraining power at work today is the authority of civil government. When that authority begins to crumble during the chaos of the Tribulation period, the stage will be set for the emergence of the Antichrist.

The Antichrist also kills the two witnesses who have been preaching the message of Jesus in Jerusalem for three and a half years. These two men were pointing out clearly that the Antichrist was an agent of Satan, not God, and they pay for their testimony with their lives. Their bodies will lie in public view for three and a half days as the world looks on and celebrates (Revelation 11:7 – 10). The people of the world will blame all the judgments and plagues of the Tribulation on these two preachers — and they will be happy to see them go. But after three and a half days, God raises them from death and takes them directly to heaven in a cloud (Revelation 11:11 – 13).

Meanwhile, back in the Temple, the Antichrist has constructed an image of himself as the object of the world's worship. The Antichrist also introduces another powerful leader — the high priest of the Antichrist's new religion. John in Revelation saw this false prophet as a second beast:

> Then I saw another beast, coming out of the earth. He had two horns like a lamb, but he spoke like a dragon. He exercised all the authority of the first beast [the Antichrist] on his behalf, and made the earth and its inhabitants worship the first beast, whose fatal wound had been healed. And he performed great and miraculous signs, even causing fire to come down from heaven to earth in full view of men. Because of the signs he was given power to do on behalf of the first beast, he deceived the inhabitants of the earth. He ordered them to set up an image in honor of the beast who was wounded by the sword and yet lived. He was given power to give breath to the image of the first beast, so that it could speak and cause all who refused to worship the image to be killed. (Revelation 13:11 – 15)

The false prophet also insists that every person under the Antichrist's authority receive a mark on their right hand or forehead. Without the mark no one will be able to hold a job, buy food, or avoid arrest and execution:

BACK TO THE DRAWING BOARD

In a *USA Today* newspaper advertisement (July 9, 2001), a group claiming to have discovered the "True Bible Code" made this prediction:

- The United Nations takes over political control of the world on or before August 23, 2001.

- The UN will be controlled by ten leaders from ten nations, starting between August 23 and November 21, 2001.

A SATANIC TRINITY

Satan does his best to imitate God — but only to accomplish evil, not good. In Revelation 13 three key figures form a satanic counterfeit of the Trinity. Christians believe in one God who exists in three persons — God the Father, God the Son (Jesus), and God the Holy Spirit. In Satan's corrupted version, Satan (called "the dragon" in Revelation 12) is the mastermind, the real power.

The second member of this unholy trinity is the Antichrist (the "beast coming out of the sea" or "the first beast"). Satan gives the Antichrist "his power and his throne and great authority" (Revelation 13:2). When men and women worship the beast, they are really worshiping Satan — something Satan has craved since he first rebelled against God and set his heart on being like God.

The third person in the confederation is the false prophet ("another beast"). Since this beast comes out of "the earth" [or "the land" of Palestine], some believe that the false prophet will be Jewish. He supervises the worship of the Antichrist and dazzles the world with his power to perform miracles. He will even empower the image of the Antichrist in the Temple so that the image itself will speak (Revelation 13:13, 15).

All three members of this alliance will be defeated and cast forever into a lake of fire (Revelation 19:20 – 21; 20:10).

He also forced everyone, small and great, rich and poor, free and slave, to receive a mark on his right hand or on his forehead, so that no one could buy or sell unless he had the mark, which is the name of the beast or the number of his name. (Revelation 13:16 – 17)

Two groups will resist the Antichrist's efforts to spread his new religion — the followers of Jesus (many of whom have come to faith through the preaching of the two witnesses) and the Jewish people. The followers of Jesus will recognize the Antichrist's evil intentions from the very beginning. When the Jewish people see the Antichrist desecrate their Temple with an image to be worshiped, they will finally recognize that he is a false leader and an enemy.

Jesus warned the Jewish people that, when they saw "the abomination" (Daniel's word for the image of the Antichrist) standing in the Temple, they were to run for their lives:

So when you see standing in the holy place "the abomination that causes desolation," spoken of through the prophet Daniel — let

666

The mark of the beast has become a universal symbol of terror and oppression — but what is it? John says that a *mark* (the word John uses means "a brand" — as in branding cattle; think *tattoo*) will be placed on the forehead or on the right hand. It is obviously a permanent mark of a person's allegiance to the Antichrist. It is also an access code that permits the person to conduct the responsibilities of life — get a job, buy food, get a driver's license, and so forth.

When Social Security numbers began to be issued to every United States citizen, some Christians were convinced that the mark of the beast had come. Internal Revenue forms, retail store bar codes, credit cards, and even Internet addresses have at one time or another been pointed to as "the mark." Technology exists today to implant microchips or "personal bar codes" invisibly on a human body. The Antichrist will certainly use whatever means are available to him to pursue his goal of total control over every person and every facet of life.

But don't leap to the conclusion that getting a Social Security number or using a bar code scanner makes you part of the Antichrist's program. When the mark *is* implemented, no one will be duped into getting one. Every person who takes on the mark of the beast will know exactly what he or she is doing. The mark will acknowledge a person's absolute allegiance to the Antichrist as political ruler and god.

John adds one more puzzling element to his description of the beast's mark. The mark will be the name of the beast or the number of his name.

> This calls for wisdom. If anyone has insight, let him calculate the number of the beast, for it is man's number. His number is 666. (Revelation 13:18)

The number of the beast's name is *man's number,* or 666. Do *you* understand that? No wonder it takes wisdom to figure it out!

John is probably referring to the ancient practice of assigning numbers to various letters of the alphabet and then calculating the "number" of a person's name. If A = 1 and B = 2 and so on through the alphabet and your name is John, the number of your name is 47 (J = 10; O = 15; H = 8; N = 14). But if A = 1 and so on until you get to 10 and then K = 20 until you get to 100, John computes to 128 (J = 10; O = 60; H = 8; N = 50).

The Antichrist's name computes to 666 — but what numerical system are we supposed to use? And what language? Christians have found "666" everywhere! Almost every year someone claims to have "discovered" how someone's name adds up to 666. Sometimes names have to be translated into Hebrew or Greek in order to get the math to come out right.

The one I remember best is the claim of some "prophetic scholar" to have figured out that

continued at top of next page

Ronald Wilson Reagan was the Antichrist because he had six letters in each of his three names — or 6/6/6. Do you really think that the apostle John had the English language in mind when he wrote this in the year A.D. 90 or so? Other speculations don't even refer to a person's name. In 1956 one Bible teacher confidently declared that John F. Kennedy was the Antichrist because he received 666 votes at the Democratic presidential convention.

My personal opinion is that no one will know how this 666 thing works until the mark begins to be branded on people's hands and foreheads. It will be obvious then, but to us right now it's still a mystery.

the reader understand — then let those who are in Judea flee to the mountains. Let no one on the roof of his house go down to take anything out of the house. Let no one in the field go back to get his cloak. How dreadful it will be in those days for pregnant women and nursing mothers! Pray that your flight will not take place in winter or on the Sabbath. For then there will be great distress, unequaled from the beginning of the world until now — and never to be equaled again. (Matthew 24:15 – 21)

A Crashing End: The Antichrist's Career — Phase Three

Because of the Antichrist's incredible personal appeal, his miraculous powers, and his political and economic control, the world falls at his feet in worship: "All inhabitants of the earth will worship the beast — all whose names have not been written in the book of life" (Revelation 13:8).

The Antichrist then determines to persecute and wipe out those who resist him — the followers of Jesus Christ and the Jews. Jesus called this last three and a half years of the Tribulation the "great tribulation" (Matthew 24:21 NASB). The Antichrist even destroys the false religious system that had helped him rise to such great power in the first years of the Tribulation (Revelation 17:1 – 18). He will tolerate no worship but the worship directed at himself.

Men and women who resist the Antichrist will be hunted down and killed, but those who support the Antichrist and receive his mark will face even greater perils. God's most punishing judgments will come

COMPUTERS AND CREDIT CARDS

The escalating use of credit cards has been widely regarded by prophecy buffs as the first step toward a universal money card that the Antichrist will use to control all buying and selling. One writer came up with this ingenious proposal: "VI" is the Roman numeral for 6; the number 6 in classical Greek "resembles" the letter S; and "it is possible" that the Babylonian letter for the A sound also had the value of 6. Put it all together and 6 + 6 + 6 spells — "VISA"! (Talk about a stretch!)

Computers have made the threat of absolute control over income and spending more of a possibility. Jerry Church figured out that if you give A the value of 6, B the value of 12, and so on, you come up with the following:

C = 18
O = 90
M = 78
P = 96
U = 126
T = 120
E = 30
R = 108

C-O-M-P-U-T-E-R adds up to 666! By the way, "Mark of the Beast" and "New York City" also total 666.

Some writers have suggested that the Antichrist will be a computer — an idea that picked up some steam when employees at the European Common Market headquarters in Luxembourg affectionately nicknamed the central computer "The Beast."

Note: These illustrations are from Paul Boyer, *When Time Shall Be No More: Prophecy Belief in Modern American Culture* (Cambridge, Mass.: Belknap/Harvard, 1992), 282 – 83.

on the earth in the last half of the Tribulation. The universe will shake loose, as judgment after judgment pounds the earth and the people on it. People will crawl into caves and wish for death — anything to protect them from the outpouring of God's anger on rebellious humanity.

The beginning of the end comes when the Antichrist hears reports of a massive army marching against him from the east — probably from China and India. Those parts of the world are the only areas not under the Antichrist's direct or indirect control (Revelation 9:13 – 16). The Antichrist will gather his own military forces in the land of Israel

Digging Deeper

✗ Hindson, Ed. *Is the Antichrist Alive and Well? 10 Keys to His Identity*. Eugene, Ore.: Harvest House, 1998.

to meet the invading army. The war that follows is called the battle of Armageddon (see chapter 6).

The Antichrist either wins this war or persuades the armies from the east to join with him against the remnants of the people of Israel who are still alive in Palestine. When the situation looks most hopeless for Israel, Jesus will return from heaven in power and glory and majesty (Matthew 24:29 – 31). The last act of the Antichrist will be his attack on the armies of the Lord: "Then I saw the beast and the kings of the earth and their armies gathered together to make war against the rider on the horse [Jesus] and his army" (Revelation 19:19).

There really isn't much of a battle! Jesus speaks a word of judgment — one puff of breath — and, like a giant sword, his spoken word destroys his enemies (Revelation 19:15, 21; 2 Thessalonians 2:8). The Antichrist is not killed in this final war. He and his sidekick, the false prophet, are cast alive into a place of eternal torment (Revelation 19:20). The rest of his army dies, and scavenging birds eat their rotting flesh (Revelation 19:21).

Points 2 Remember

- ☑ The Antichrist is a future ruler who will dominate the world during the seven-year Tribulation period.

- ☑ He will announce that he is a god and demand the worship of every person.

- ☑ The Antichrist will be empowered by Satan.

- ☑ The Antichrist and his empire will be destroyed by the return of Jesus from heaven in magnificent glory.

- ☑ The *power* of the Antichrist is at work in our world today; the *person* of the Antichrist will be revealed in the future when God no longer holds back Satan's evil plans.

HELP FILE
SATAN'S LAST STAND

There he stands at your front door on a crisp October night — red horns, pointed tail, red pitchfork — Satan looking for a Halloween handout! Not! But unfortunately that's how some people think of Satan — as a harmless little imp, a prankster, a Halloween boogeyman.

Other people give Satan way too much power. They see him behind every bad experience and the cause of every pothole in the road. It's as though God and Satan are punching it out and these folks really aren't sure who's going to win.

It is certainly dangerous to think of Satan as just a Halloween character. Satan is in fact a powerful angel who turned against God and set out on a course of rebellion against and hatred toward God. Other angels followed him in his rebellion and now work with Satan to oppose and destroy all that God does.

But don't give Satan too much power either. He is not equal with God — or even close. Satan operates only with God's permission. He was defeated forever by Jesus at the cross and the empty tomb. The war is over, and Satan's defeat is certain; the only thing left to do is the mop-up operation.

When Christians are removed from the earth at the rapture, God the Holy Spirit takes his hands off the wickedness in human hearts.

Today human evil is restrained. As bad as it seems to get sometimes, it's not nearly as bad as it someday will be. During the Tribulation, humankind's depravity will run full tilt.

In the middle of the Tribulation, Satan is cast out of heaven and confined to the earth (Revelation 12:7 – 13). Today Satan has access to heaven, where he accuses us before God. In the future Satan's access will be revoked. Satan and his accomplice, the Antichrist, will seek out and destroy as many believers in Jesus as they can during the Tribulation. Satan will also seek to destroy the people of Israel, for God has promises yet to fulfill to Israel.

When Jesus returns in power, the Antichrist is thrown alive into the lake of fire (Revelation 19:20). Satan is confined in a dreadful place called the Abyss, or bottomless pit (Revelation 20:1 – 3). He spends a thousand years in darkness and bondage.

At the end of the Kingdom Age, Satan is released for a time, and he sweeps all those who have not believed in Jesus into one final rebellious mob. The rebels are destroyed and Satan is cast into the lake of fire (Revelation 20:10). Even Satan will bow his knee to Jesus and confess that Jesus is Lord (Philippians 2:8 – 11) — and then he will be banished to hell forever.

CHAPTER 5

The Great Disappearance:
The Rapture

The Great Disappearance: The Rapture

Heads Up

▸ Be amazed at Jesus' return from heaven!
▸ Find out why millions of Christians could vanish tomorrow
▸ Explore three views of *when* the rapture will happen
▸ Discover how you can be "rapture-ready"

You've seen the bumper sticker: IN CASE OF RAPTURE, THIS VEHICLE WILL BE UNMANNED! Okay — but what does *that* mean?!

The rapture is a future event predicted in the Bible in which Jesus will return from heaven and gather his followers and take them into heaven. If you've never heard of the rapture, it sounds a little weird, but I want you to know that Christians didn't just dream this up. We believe in the rapture because the Bible clearly teaches that it will happen.

The passage quoted most often about the rapture is 1 Thessalonians 4:16 – 17.

> For the Lord himself will come down from heaven, with a loud command, with the voice of the archangel and with the trumpet call of God, and the dead in Christ will rise first. After that, we who are still alive and are left will be caught up together with them in the clouds to meet the Lord in the air. And so we will be with the Lord forever.

On This We Can Agree

Christians are in amazing agreement about the *fact* of the rapture, because the Bible talks directly about it. Jesus told his followers just before his death and resurrection that he would be leaving them to go back to heaven. But he also assured them that he would come back for them: "I will come back and take you to be with me that you also may be where I am" (John 14:3). After Jesus' resurrection from the dead and his ascension (going up) into heaven, two angels told his followers

Techno-Speak

Rapture

You won't find the word *rapture* anywhere in the Bible. The word comes from a Latin translation of 1 Thessalonians 4:16 – 17. In verse 17 the words "caught up" were translated *rapturo* in the Latin Bible — and we morphed that word into the English word "rapture."

that "this same Jesus, who has been taken from you into heaven, will come back in the same way you have seen him go into heaven" (Acts 1:11).

The apostle Paul is the New Testament writer who gives us the most detail about the rapture. His teaching on the subject arose from a very practical problem in one of the Christian communities he had founded. Paul had talked about Jesus in the Greek city of Thessalonica (thess-a-low-**nigh**-ka), and some of the people there had committed themselves to be followers of Jesus. Paul only spent a few weeks with these folks before he had to leave their city, but while he was there he told them about Jesus' return. These Christians looked forward to that event with great anticipation.

But after Paul left, a few of the older Christians died. That made the other Christians wonder about what would happen to their friends when Jesus came back. Would those who had died be left out of the glory of Jesus' return?

Paul addresses their concerns in the first letter he wrote to them — a letter we call 1 Thessalonians:

> Brothers, we do not want you to be ignorant about those who fall asleep [meaning, about those who die], or to grieve like the rest of men, who have no hope. We believe that Jesus died and rose again and so we believe that God will bring with Jesus those who have fallen asleep in him. According to the Lord's own word, we tell you that we who are still alive, who are left till the coming of the Lord, will certainly not precede those who have fallen asleep. (1 Thessalonians 4:13 – 15)

Those who die as believers in Jesus will not be left behind when Jesus returns. Their bodies "sleep" in the grave, but their spirits, the real people inside those bodies, go to be with the Lord in heaven. When Jesus comes back to take his followers out of the world, he will bring back with him all those who have died. They will be part of the event. They won't miss out on seeing Jesus rescue his people from the earth.

But something else will happen to those who have died. Their bodies, which have been buried and have crumbled to dust, will be resurrected — returned to life, just like Jesus' body was raised back to life. And the bodies will be changed. Christians who have died will have a body like Jesus' resurrection body, a body that will not age or decay or die, a body built for eternity.

Christians who are still alive when Jesus returns will not experience physical death. We will be "caught up" (raptured) and our bodies will be instantly changed. We will be taken out of the world into heaven to be with Jesus forever.

When you scroll through this list of events — Jesus returns, archangel's voice, dead Christians raised to life, living Christians changed and taken out of the world — it sounds as if it could take days or weeks to get it all done. According to the Bible, however, it will all be over in a split second:

> Listen, I tell you a mystery: We will not all sleep [that is, not all Christians will experience physical death], but we will all be changed — in a flash, in the twinkling of an eye, at the last trumpet. For the trumpet will sound, the dead will be raised imperishable, and we will be changed. (1 Corinthians 15:51 – 52)

IN A FLASH

People who like to figure these things out claim that "the twinkling of an eye" (1 Corinthians 15:52) is about one-thousandth of a second. When Paul says that all Christians who are alive at the time of the rapture will be changed "in a flash," he uses the Greek word *atomos*, from which we get our word "atom." The rapture will take place in the smallest division of time — one "atom" of time. In a flash, every living follower of Christ will be gone.

What impresses me as I read what Paul wrote about the rapture is that he fully expected to be one of the Christians still alive when Jesus returned. In 1 Thessalonians 4:17 he said that *we* who are still alive and are left will be caught up. In 1 Corinthians 15:51 he said that *we* will all be changed.

Christians often say that they believe Jesus will return soon. Our parents and grandparents believed it, too. In fact, *every* generation of Christians has looked expectantly for the rapture. That's because the Bible teaches that Jesus could return at any time. Paul thought it would happen in his lifetime. He was wrong, but his anticipation was not wrong. We are challenged to live every moment as though it could be the moment when Jesus returns.

So the bumper sticker is accurate! If the rapture took place as you drove behind a Christian's car, the driver would be taken out of the world in an instant. When Jesus returns for his followers, millions of Christians will be caught up to meet the Lord.

When Will All This Happen?

Christians are in basic agreement on the *fact* of the rapture, but we have very different views on *when* the rapture will take place.

If you have read the popular Left Behind series of futuristic novels by Tim LaHaye and Jerry Jenkins, you might conclude that their view of how future events will unfold is the only view held by the Christian community. But this is *not* the case — for one simple reason. While there are clear statements in the Bible telling us *what* the rapture will be like, there is no clear, definitive statement telling us *when* it will occur. Every view on the time of the rapture is based on hints and

Techno-Speak

Imminent

The biblical teaching that Jesus could return at any moment is called "the imminent return of Christ." The word *imminent* means "close, soon, unannounced."

JESUS IS COMING! OCTOBER 21 — OR MAYBE OCTOBER 22 — OR MAYBE . . .

- On New Year's Eve, A.D. 999, Pope Sylvester II celebrated what he thought would be the last mass of history. He based his view on Revelation 20:7 – 8, which he thought predicted a one-thousand-year Church Age until Jesus returned. Across Europe people had given away money and homes to the poor. Thousands of pilgrims flocked to Jerusalem, hoping to see Jesus descend from heaven. As midnight approached in Rome, Pope Sylvester raised his hands to heaven. The bells rang in the year 1000, but Jesus did not return.

- Edgar C. Whisenant predicted that Jesus would return in September of 1988. Several million copies of his book *88 Reasons Why the Rapture Will Be in 1988* were sold. When September 1988 passed, Whisenant published a revised edition of his book and reset the date for October 3, 1989.

- In 1990 Elizabeth Clare Prophet, a New Age visionary who claims to communicate directly with Jesus and Buddha, issued a call to her followers to the "Church Universal and Triumphant" compound in Montana. She predicted that a nuclear war would destroy everyone except her faithful flock. Thousands of people sold their possessions and moved to Paradise Valley. When the date of history's final war passed without incident, the cult leader claimed that her prayers had averted the disaster.

- Harold Camping went on his network of Christian radio stations in 1992 to announce that Jesus would return between September 15 and 27, 1994. Donations to his radio stations and newly formed church poured in. When September 27, 1994, passed, Camping simply said that he had miscalculated.

clues drawn from the Bible, but no one can point to a Scripture verse that says exactly when Jesus will come. Some views have a stronger biblical foundation than other views, but no single view answers every biblical question.

It really isn't accurate to say that Christians know when the rapture will take place. We can only try to place the time of the rapture in relation to other future events. The main question about the time of the rapture is when will it occur *in relation to* the Tribulation — will it be before the Tribulation or at the end or somewhere in the middle?

(See the chapter on the Tribulation for a full discussion of this future time of God's judgment on a world that has rejected him.)

If someone comes along and says that they know *the date* of Jesus' return, put their book back on the shelf, turn to another television channel, or click on another Web site. The Bible says that NO ONE knows the exact time, date, season, or year of Jesus' return. When he was on earth, Jesus himself didn't even know the date of his return! Here's what he says: "No one knows about that day or hour, not even the angels in heaven, nor the Son, but only the Father" (Matthew 24:36). Even after his resurrection, when his disciples asked him to give them a timetable for his return, Jesus said, "It is not for you to know the times or dates the Father has set by his own authority" (Acts 1:7).

Many people have tried to figure out the date of Jesus' return — and thousands of Christians have been swept into believing these date-setters. But they have all been wrong!

In the next few pages I've summarized the three main views on the time of the rapture, along with what I see as the strengths and weaknesses of each view. In the end, you will have to decide which view you think is most consistent with the biblical evidence.

Rapture Timeline #1: The Rapture Will Occur <u>Before</u> the Seven-Year Tribulation

Many Christians believe that the rapture will be the event that marks the beginning of the Tribulation period. This view is called the "pretribulation rapture" view — or "pretrib" in Christian lingo.

Here's how pretribulation people see future events unfolding:

- Jesus will return in the air to take Christians out of the world. Christians who have died are raised to life and living Christians are caught up to meet the Lord.
- Shortly after the rapture, world events take a dramatic turn for the worse. God begins to bring judgment and catastrophe on the world, and corrupt nations begin their campaigns of war and terror. Over the course of seven years, God allows human civilization to collapse under the weight of his judgment.

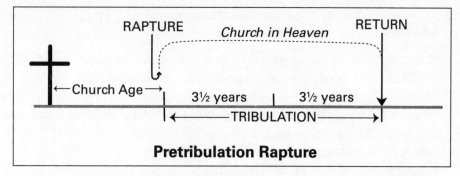

Pretribulation Rapture

- At the end of the Tribulation, Jesus returns to the earth in majesty and power. Christians (who have been in heaven during the Tribulation) return with Jesus and witness his final defeat of the Antichrist.
- Jesus then sweeps evil people and the remnants of all human government from the earth and sets up a Kingdom of peace.

Arguments for the Defense

Proponents of the pretribulation rapture use the following arguments to support their position:

1. The Bible promises that true followers of Christ will be rescued out of the horrors of the Tribulation.

Key verses are

Revelation 3:10 — Jesus is talking to the faithful believers in the Christian community:

> Since you have kept my command to endure patiently, I will also keep you from the hour of trial that is going to come upon the whole world to test those who live on the earth.

First Thessalonians 5:9 — Paul is talking about Jesus' return and the coming "day of the Lord" (5:1):

> For God did not appoint us to suffer wrath but to receive salvation through our Lord Jesus Christ.

God's promise is that we will not suffer his wrath, his anger against sin. We will not have to experience it in eternity, and we will not experience it during the Tribulation. Instead we will be rescued and delivered from God's wrath.

CLOUDS

Whenever God shows up in visible form in the Bible, he is usually surrounded by clouds of glory — and clouds are part of Jesus' return, too. The apostle Paul says that at the rapture Christians will be caught up "in the clouds" (1 Thessalonians 4:17). When Jesus returns to earth to set up his Kingdom, the world will "see the Son of Man coming on the clouds of the sky, with power and great glory" (Matthew 24:30). When Jesus was taken up to heaven forty days after his resurrection, "a cloud hid him from their sight" (Acts 1:9). Clouds were the mark of God's presence and power.

First Thessalonians 1:10 makes the same promise:

> [You, Christians, are waiting] for his Son from heaven, whom he raised from the dead — Jesus, who rescues us from the coming wrath.

2. The "church," or community of Christians, is not pictured on earth during the Tribulation. In the book of Revelation, the apostle John gives a lot of detail about the Tribulation in chapters 6 – 19, but he only talks about the church in chapters 1 – 3. Then he pictures the church in heaven in chapters 4 and 5. (The "twenty-four elders" seated around God's throne in Revelation 4:4 is usually understood to refer to Christians who have been taken to heaven.) John does not refer to the church as being on earth again until the end of the Tribulation when "the bride" (an image used in the New Testament for the followers of Jesus) returns from heaven with Jesus (Revelation 19:7 – 8, 14).

3. Christians are told to expect the rapture at any time. As we've already seen, the New Testament writers anticipated the return of Jesus at any moment (click on 1 Corinthians 15:51 – 52; 1 Thessalonians 4:16 – 17; and Titus 2:13). Their expectation suggests that the rapture will be the *first* event to occur. If the rapture comes at the end of the Tribulation, it won't be a surprise. Christians could calculate the time of the rapture several years in advance.

4. None of the New Testament letters contain a warning to Christians that they will go through the future Tribulation. All the biblical passages used by those who think Christians will go through the Tribulation (or part of it) come from the Gospels or the book of Revelation.

I Beg to Differ . . .

The evidence for the pretribulation rapture sounds pretty convincing — but Christians who hold other views about the time of the rapture have raised some interesting questions for their pretrib friends.

1. The promises in the Bible about being delivered from the wrath of God refer to God's *eternal* wrath on our sin, not to the suffering we may experience on earth. In fact, the Bible specifically says that in this age Christians will suffer persecution from the world (John 16:33; Acts 14:22). Jesus also told two of the churches in Revelation 2 – 3 that they would experience "tribulation" and even "great tribulation" (Revelation 2:10, 22 NASB). To expect God to rapture us out of the world before the Tribulation is to read too much into the biblical promises.

2. There are Scripture passages that seem to suggest that the New Testament writers did *not* expect Jesus' return at any moment. Jesus, for example, told Peter that Peter would die in his old age (John 21:18 – 19). Jesus also predicted that the city of Jerusalem would be destroyed.

JESUS HAS ALREADY COME!

William Miller, a Baptist preacher, believed that he had discovered the secret of determining the date of Jesus' return and the end of the world. Reluctantly at first, and then to growing crowds, Miller announced that Jesus would return between March 21, 1843 and March 21, 1844.

When the dates passed without incident, many Millerites (as his followers were called) left the movement. Others simply set new dates. One of Miller's followers, Ellen G. White, began to teach that Jesus had come in a "spiritual" sense on October 22, 1844. Jesus had come into the heavenly sanctuary but was delaying his coming to earth because so many Christians were not keeping the Ten Commandments, especially the fourth one — the command to worship on the Sabbath, or the seventh day of the week. In time, the Seventh-day Adventist movement was born.

Charles Russell led another group of Miller's followers. Russell calculated the date of Jesus' return as 1878. When Jesus did not come to earth, Russell claimed that Jesus had made a spiritual return to the "upper air" of the earth. He then concluded that Jesus would set up his kingdom on earth in 1914. Until then, true followers of Jehovah (an Old Testament name for God — from the Hebrew name *Yahweh*) were to become faithful witnesses to the world — and the Jehovah's Witness movement began.

BACK TO THE DRAWING BOARD

Joseph Smith, the founder of Mormonism, wrote this prediction in his diary, dated April 6, 1843: "I prophesy in the name of the Lord God — and let it be written: that the Son of Man will not come in the heavens till I am 85 years old, 48 years hence, or about 1890." Joseph Smith was murdered in 1844 — one year after making the prediction.

In *I Predict 2000 A.D.*, Lester Sumrall claimed the year 2000 to be the date of Jesus' return. "I predict the absolute fullness of man's operation on planet Earth by the year 2000 A.D. Then Jesus Christ will reign from Jerusalem for 1000 years."

Christopher Columbus believed that he would fulfill prophecy through his explorations. He envisioned raising up a Christian army that would convert the world to Christianity. By his calculations the world would end in 1656.

That didn't happen until A.D. 70 — years after all of Paul's letters had been written and both Paul and Peter had been executed.

3. While the book of Revelation never refers to the "church" on earth during the Tribulation, it does talk about "saints" and a great multitude in heaven who had "come out of the great tribulation" (7:14) — clearly followers of Jesus who were killed for their faith *during* the Tribulation.

Rapture Timeline #2:
The Rapture Will Occur <u>During</u> the Seven-Year Tribulation

Sometimes this view is called the "midtribulation rapture" view or the "prewrath rapture." Here's how events unfold in this version of the future:

- Christians will go through part of the Tribulation — probably the first three and a half years of the seven-year Tribulation.
- Three series of judgments from God come upon the earth during the Tribulation:
  1. Seven judgments, as Jesus breaks seven wax seals on a scroll in heaven (Revelation 6:1 – 17; 8:1)
  2. Seven new judgments (more severe than the first), as seven angels blow trumpets in heaven (Revelation 8:2 – 9:21; 11:15 – 19)

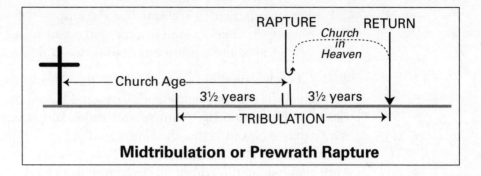

Midtribulation or Prewrath Rapture

   3. Seven final catastrophic judgments, as seven angels in heaven
      pour out bowls of God's wrath on the earth (Revelation
      15:1 – 16:17)

- When the seventh angel blows the seventh trumpet (Revelation
  11:15), Jesus will return in the air and take Christians out of the
  world.
- Those who are left on earth during the last half of the Tribulation
  will experience God's wrath. At the end of the Tribulation, Jesus will
  return in power to destroy the Antichrist and set up his own Kingdom of peace.

All in Favor . . .

Those Christians who believe that Jesus will come during the Tribulation base their view on the following biblical evidence:

1. Jesus promised that the time of tribulation would be "shortened" for
his followers.

> For then there will be great distress, unequaled from the beginning
> of the world until now — and never to be equaled again. If those days
> had not been cut short, no one would survive, but for the sake of the
> elect those days will be shortened. (Matthew 24:21 – 22)

2. The Bible promises that Christians will be delivered from God's
wrath, not from the Tribulation itself. Since the seven bowl judgments
in Revelation are specifically called "the seven bowls of God's wrath"
(Revelation 16:1; see 15:7), Christians are raptured just *before* the bowl
judgments begin. (This is where the phrase "prewrath rapture" comes
from.)

3. Paul in 1 Corinthians 15:52 says that the rapture will take place "at the last trumpet." The seventh trumpet judgment seems to be the last trumpet — and so the rapture must take place at that point.

4. The church *is* pictured on earth during the Tribulation. In Revelation 11:4 John refers to "two lampstands that stand before the Lord of the earth." In Revelation 1:20, churches are called lampstands, and it seems reasonable to conclude that the lampstands in Revelation 11 also represent churches. The two lampstands in Revelation 11 are attacked by the Antichrist but are then taken up "to heaven in a cloud, while their ene-

CRACKING THE BIBLE CODE

Every few months a new book comes out that claims to have found astonishing messages hidden in the Bible — and it's not just Christians or prophecy geeks who make these claims. Jewish rabbis and secular linguists have taken a shot at it as well.

The basic belief is that there are hidden codes in the Hebrew text of the Old Testament. Computers are used to search for letters that occur at specific intervals or spaces. The process is called Equidistant Letter Sequencing (ELS). The researcher finds a Hebrew letter, skips three letters, takes that letter, skips three more, and so on. Eventually hidden words or short messages are revealed. Bible code researchers claim to have found references to Hitler, John Kennedy, New York City — as well as many references to Jesus—in the Old Testament.

I've never been very impressed with this whole process for several reasons. First, the skip distances are never the same. Sometimes they skip three letters at a time to find a hidden message; other messages are found by skipping ten letters at a time.

Second, Bible code computers have also found more than two thousand references to Muhammad in the Old Testament — and over one hundred references to Krishna (a Hindu god). Hearing this doesn't give me much confidence that these are secret messages from God.

Third, you can apply the same technique to any book and get some kind of hidden message. Michael Drosnin, author of *The Bible Code*, issued a memorable challenge: "When my critics find a message or name related to the assassination of a world leader in *Moby Dick*, I'll believe them." Professor Brendan McKay, a mathematician at the Australian National University, using the same technique on Melville's *Moby Dick*, found thirteen hidden words related to assassinations — Indira Gandhi, Martin Luther King Jr., Sirhan Sirhan, John F. Kennedy, Abraham Lincoln, and Yitzhak Rabin (reported in *Newsweek*, 9 June 1997, 67).

My suggestion: Stick to reading the Bible, and forget any hidden codes. They don't exist!

mies looked on" (Revelation 11:12). This seems like a clear reference to the rapture, and it takes place in the middle of the Tribulation.

I Object!

Christians who hold different viewpoints about the rapture have raised some serious questions about the midtrib/prewrath view.

1. The *entire* seven-year period of the Tribulation is referred to as the time of God's wrath. Revelation 6:16 – 17 describes a time early in the seven-year Tribulation, and yet people on earth cry out to the mountains and rocks and say, "Fall on us and hide us from the face of him who sits on the throne [God] and from the wrath of the Lamb! For the great day of their wrath has come, and who can stand?"

WHAT AMERICANS THINK . . .

- 62 percent have no doubts that Jesus will return again.
- 52 percent are convinced that they will give an answer to God for their sins.
- In 1994, 16 percent thought that the world would end within the next hundred years.
- In 1991, 15 percent believed that the Gulf War was the fulfillment of the biblical prediction of the decisive battle of Armageddon.

2. Paul's reference to "the last trumpet" means the trumpet call that will accompany the rapture (1 Thessalonians 4:16; Revelation 4:1), *not* the seventh trumpet judgment in the middle of the Tribulation. There is no clear indication in Revelation 11:15 – 19 that the rapture occurs at that point.

3. The two lampstands in Revelation 11 clearly refer to two human beings, not churches. These witnesses for God during the Tribulation are killed by the Antichrist but are raised to life by God and then are taken to heaven (Revelation 11:7 – 12).

Rapture Timeline #3: The Rapture Will Occur at the <u>End</u> of the Seven-Year Tribulation

Some Christians have looked at the biblical evidence and concluded that the church will go through the entire Tribulation. This position is called the (you guessed it!) "posttribulation rapture" view.

The future scenario, according to posttribulationists, looks like this:

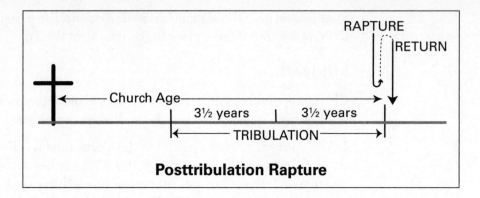

Posttribulation Rapture

- The world will continue its downward spiral into violence and evil until God brings his final judgment in the form of seven years of great Tribulation.
- Christians will increasingly be persecuted. During the Tribulation, the Antichrist will mount one final campaign against Jesus' followers and will be at the point of total victory. Jesus will return at that moment to destroy the Antichrist and rescue God's faithful people.
- Dead Christians will be raised to life. Living Christians will be changed and taken up into the air. Then all of God's church, all the Christians of every generation, will return immediately with Jesus in victory.

Posttrib Strengths

1. The Bible indicates that Christians will experience serious persecution and suffering in the present age. Jesus in John 16:33 says, "In this world you will have trouble. But take heart! I have overcome the world." Or how about Paul and Barnabas in Acts 14:22: "We must go through many hardships to enter the kingdom of God."

2. Jesus in Revelation says that he will cast some of the Christians into great tribulation: "Do not fear what you are about to suffer. Behold, the devil is about to cast some of you into prison, so that you will be tested, and you will have tribulation for ten days. Be faithful until death, and I will give you the crown of life" (Revelation 2:10 NASB). And again, "Behold, I will throw her on a bed of sickness, and those who commit adultery with her into great tribulation, unless they repent of her deeds" (Revelation 2:22 NASB).

3. The Bible's promises that we will be rescued from God's wrath refer only to God's *eternal* judgment against our sin. We *will* be delivered from hell but not from suffering on earth at the hands of God's enemies.

4. Jesus taught that Christians would be on earth when the Antichrist sets up his own image in the temple in Jerusalem, an event that occurs in the middle of the Tribulation (Mark 13:14 – 23). Jesus also pointed to his return in glory at the end of the Tribulation as the event we should be looking for as Christians:

> At that time men will see the Son of Man coming in clouds with great power and glory....
>
> Be on guard! Be alert! You do not know when that time will come....
>
> Therefore keep watch because you do not know when the owner of the house will come back — whether in the evening, or at midnight, or when the rooster crows, or at dawn. If he comes suddenly, do not let him find you sleeping. What I say to you, I say to everyone: "Watch!"
>
> (Mark 13:26, 33, 35 – 37)

5. Some passages of Scripture seem to imply that the New Testament writers did not expect Jesus to return at any moment. Jesus told Peter that Peter would die in his old age (John 21:18 – 19). Some of Jesus' parables and other teachings suggest that a long period of time will intervene between Jesus' first coming and his second coming (Matthew 13:1 – 50; 28:19 – 20; Luke 19:11 – 17; Matthew 25:14 – 30). Furthermore, Jesus predicted that Jerusalem would be destroyed (Matthew 24:2), an event that had not yet happened when Paul wrote his New

PRESERVED OR PROTECTED?

Advocates of the posttribulation rapture are divided on whether Christians will be protected from suffering during the Tribulation or whether they will suffer God's judgment along with the rest of humanity. On one hand, God at times has preserved and protected his people from the suffering that others experienced (Noah and his family were sheltered in the ark from the flood; the Israelites in slavery in Egypt did not suffer the full weight of God's plagues). On the other hand, thousands of Christians have been persecuted and even suffered death as martyrs through the centuries. Why should Christians expect to be protected during the coming catastrophe?

PARTIAL RAPTURE

You may encounter one more view of the rapture — a "partial rapture" view. This teaching says that the rapture will come before the Tribulation, but only *prepared* Christians will be taken out. Unprepared Christians who are not fully following Jesus will remain and will face the difficulties of the Tribulation. This has never been a popular view among Christians because it doesn't have much biblical support. The passage usually identified as supporting this position is Jesus' story about the ten virgins in Matthew 25:1 – 13. Five of the virgins were prepared for the bridegroom's coming and were taken into the celebration. The five who were unprepared missed the bridegroom's coming and were left outside.

Testament letters. How could Jesus return to earth before his prediction about Jerusalem was fulfilled?

Only "Post"-Toasties!

The posttribulation rapture view has also come under the scrutiny of Christians who hold different views. They raise some interesting points:

1. Scripture's statements about the church experiencing tribulation or suffering refer to times of persecution or opposition that Christians have endured throughout the entire span of time since Jesus was here. Those statements are not referring to the final Tribulation period.

2. The posttribulation rapture view contradicts the biblical teaching that Jesus could return for his followers at any moment. If Jesus won't come until the end of the seven-year Tribulation, Christians at some point will be able to calculate exactly when he will return. The parables that imply a long period of time between Jesus' first coming and his second coming also contain warnings about being ready for his return at any moment. Jesus' predictions about Peter's old

Points 2 Remember

☑ The rapture is an event predicted in the Bible in which Jesus will return from heaven and take all Christians, living and dead, to be with him forever.

☑ The Bible tells us that no one (except God) knows the precise time of Jesus' return. Don't be duped by someone who says he or she has it all figured out.

☑ Christians agree on the *fact* of Jesus' return but disagree on *when* the rapture will occur in relation to other future events.

age and about Jerusalem's destruction do not rule out Jesus' imminent return. The prediction could still have been fulfilled in God's plan. No specific length of time was attached to Jesus' predictions or to the length of the present age.

3. Jesus' teaching in Mark and Matthew was given to his disciples before the New Testament teaching on the rapture was made clear. Jesus did not explain how events would unfold. We have to merge the New Testament teaching that the rapture will take place before the Tribulation with the things that Jesus taught.

Finding the Right Path

Three views. Each one is held by sincere Christians who base their conclusions on the Bible. There's only one problem. Who's right?

Let me warn you that you could spend years studying the intricate details of these differing views (and several variations of each of these views). Lots of Christians have become stuck on one point or one

DigginG DeEpeR

An interesting overview:

✗ Archer, Gleason L. Jr., Paul D. Feinberg, Douglas J. Moo, and Richard R. Reiter. *Three Views on the Rapture: Pre-, Mid-, or Post-Tribulational?* Grand Rapids: Zondervan, 1984, 1996.

On the *pretribulation* rapture position:

✗ Ryrie, Charles. *What You Should Know about the Rapture.* Chicago: Moody Press, 1981.

On the *prewrath* rapture position:

✗ Rosenthal, Marvin. *The Prewrath Rapture of the Church.* Nashville: Nelson, 1990.

On the *posttribulation* rapture position:

✗ Gundry, Bob. *First the Antichrist.* Grand Rapids: Baker, 1997.

✗ Kimball, William. *The Rapture: A Question of Timing.* Grand Rapids: Baker, 1985.

view. My suggestion is to study the biblical evidence for each view and come to your own conclusion. But be sure to hold that view with a little humility. The fact that God has not made one position crystal clear in Scripture should make us all listen more closely to the views of other Christians. I personally believe that the rapture will come *before* the Tribulation begins. I think the biblical evidence for this position is more compelling than the evidence used to support the other positions. You may disagree with me — but we can still be friends!

Instead of arguing tirelessly about the different views, keep your focus on the central truth: Jesus *is* coming back — and as Christians we are called to live every moment in that light. So seize the day, and live in eager expectation of Jesus' return!

CHAPTER 6

The Last World War:
The Battle of Armageddon

The Last World War:
The Battle of Armageddon

‣ Witness the mother of all wars

‣ Just when it looks like the wrong side will win, Jesus intervenes!

‣ The Antichrist is crushed — and condemned

If you thought that the world was going to be spared from Armageddon because Bruce Willis blew up that asteroid just in time, you are sadly mistaken! (Click on the 1998 movie *Armageddon* if you don't get the Bruce Willis line.) The word *Armageddon* has come to mean "the end of the world" in popular jargon. The word actually comes from the Bible, and it isn't the end of the world — but it does change everything.

Armageddon is a Hebrew word that means "hill of Megiddo" (*har*, which means "mountain or hill" plus *mageddon* meaning "Megiddo"; in English it becomes *Armageddon*). You will find the word only once in the Bible:

> Then I saw three evil spirits that looked like frogs; they came out of the mouth of the dragon, out of the mouth of the beast and out of the

FROM JESUS' WINDOW

The plain of Esdraelon is a triangular valley bounded by mountain ranges and the Mediterranean Sea. The city of Nazareth, where Jesus grew up, is located on the northern rim of the valley. Jesus would often have looked out over this valley as he scanned south toward the city of Megiddo. The plain is about fifteen miles wide and twenty miles long.

Some of the fiercest battles of the Old Testament were fought in this valley — Gideon's victory over the Midianite invaders (Judges 7); King Saul's defeat by the Philistines (1 Samuel 31); King Josiah's defeat by the Egyptians (2 Kings 23:29). It will also be the scene of the first battle in a great war at the end of the seven-year Tribulation — the battle of Armageddon.

mouth of the false prophet. They are spirits of demons performing miraculous signs, and they go out to the kings of the whole world, to gather them for the battle on the great day of God Almighty....

Then they gather the kings together to the place that in Hebrew is called Armageddon. (Revelation 16:13 – 14, 16)

The hill of Megiddo overlooks a wide fertile plain called the plain of Esdraelon (**ez**-dra-lon), or the valley of Jezreel. The Bible pinpoints that area as the location of "the battle on the great day of God Almighty" (Revelation 16:14). The plain of Esdraelon is located in the northern part of the land of Israel about twenty miles southeast of present-day Haifa.

John the apostle, who wrote the book of Revelation, isn't the only biblical writer to talk about this event. Daniel, Joel, and Zechariah (all Old Testament prophets) also give us information about the final battle between good and evil, between Christ and Antichrist. Military powers from all over the world will converge on one little piece of real estate. They will meet to fight each other but will end up fighting the greatest power of all, namely, Jesus Christ.

The Play-by-Play

Here's how the events will unfold: At the midpoint of the Tribulation, the Antichrist invades the land of Israel and declares himself to be a

HORSES? WHERE ARE THE FIGHTER JETS?

The Bible's description of the battle of Armageddon implies that soldiers will be on horseback and will use ancient weapons in hand-to-hand combat. Can this be an accurate description of a war still in the future?

Two possible explanations:

- The devastating wars earlier in the Tribulation and the pounding judgment of God on the world will have effectively destroyed humanity's ability to use modern technology.
- It's also possible that the biblical writers were trying to describe modern weapons with an ancient vocabulary. They had no word for tank or cruise missile!

I BEG TO DIFFER . . .

Christians have different views of the battle of Armageddon based on their approach to biblical prophecy in general. Here's a summary of other perspectives:

Historicist: Those interpreters who see the book of Revelation as picturing the unfolding of Christian and world history from Jesus' day to the present day believe that the reference to the battle of Armageddon in Revelation 16 was fulfilled in World War I. The Turkish Empire (the old Ottoman Empire that had its roots in the Euphrates River) was defeated by the British army, and Jerusalem came under western control. Historicist writers also see the Russian Revolution in 1917 as one of the unclean spirits that went out to deceive the nations.

Preterist: Interpreters who believe that the prophecies about the Tribulation were fulfilled when Rome destroyed Jerusalem in A.D. 70 see the battle of Armageddon as the decisive battle in which Roman troops broke into the city of Jerusalem and began the process of slaughtering the inhabitants. Another preterist view is that Armageddon is the spiritual battle in the hearts of early Christians between loyalty to Jesus and loyalty to the Roman Empire, the conflict between the worship of Jesus and the worship of Caesar.

Spiritual: Christians who view the book of Revelation as a symbolic picture of the constant struggle between good and evil interpret the battle of Armageddon as the final triumph of Jesus Christ over all the evil forces in the universe.

god. He demands the world's worship and allegiance (Revelation 13:1 – 2, 8; 2 Thessalonians 2:4).

The nations of the east not under the Antichrist's direct control (nations like China, India, and the Islamic nations of central and southeast Asia) agree to march against the armies of the Antichrist. The Antichrist's threat of world domination will be greater than the religious and political issues that have divided those nations for centuries.

A massive army of two hundred million people begins to move from the east toward the Antichrist's new capital in Jerusalem (Revelation 9:13 – 21). God even helps prepare the way for this army by drying up the Euphrates River (Revelation 16:12). When this enormous army reaches the area of Israel, the Antichrist will have already assembled his own army near the wide plain of Esdraelon (Daniel 11:44; Joel 3:2, 13 – 16).

Bible NetWorking

Key Bible Passages on the World's Final War

Psalm 2	Isaiah 34:1 – 5	Isaiah 63:1 – 6
Joel 3:1 – 17	Zechariah 12:1 – 9	Malachi 4:1 – 3
Revelation 14:14 – 20	Revelation 16:12 – 16	Revelation 19:19 – 21

The battle that follows is bloody. Blood from human beings and animals will literally flow like a stream through the valley. The Antichrist apparently emerges victorious over the armies of the east. It is also possible that all the armies simply decide to join forces against Jesus Christ, who is about to return (Matthew 24:29 – 30; Psalm 2:1 – 5).

The Antichrist then turns his forces against the Jews living in the land of Israel. The war that erupts from the first battle in the north eventually engulfs the whole nation. Hundreds of thousands of Jews are killed (Zechariah 12:1 – 3; 13:8 – 9; 14:1 – 2).

A small surviving group of Jews (a "remnant" preserved by God) will escape from the city of Jerusalem and flee into the desert southeast of the city. This remnant will call on God to send his Messiah to protect them (Matthew 24:16 – 28; Hosea 6:1 – 3).

Jesus will return from heaven in brilliant glory and awesome power as God's great Warrior. He will destroy the armies of the Antichrist with one word of command, one breath of his mouth. A plague will sweep over the soldiers, and their flesh will instantly rot on their bones.

The Bible puts it this way:

> Then the LORD will go out and fight against those nations, as he fights in the day of battle. On that day his feet will stand on the Mount of Olives, east of Jerusalem, and the Mount of Olives will be split in two

from east to west.... Then the LORD my God will come, and all the holy ones with him. (Zechariah 14:3, 5)

Then I saw the beast and the kings of the earth and their armies gathered together to make war against the rider on the horse [Jesus] and his army. But the beast was captured, and with him the false prophet.... The two of them were thrown alive into the fiery lake of burning sulfur. The rest of them were killed with the sword that came out of the mouth of the rider on the horse, and all the birds gorged themselves on their flesh. (Revelation 19:19 – 21)

See also Zechariah 14:12; Isaiah 63:6; Habakkuk 3:11 – 15.

The surviving Jews will recognize Jesus as their true Messiah and will turn to him in repentance and faith. The prophet Zechariah writes as follows:

And I will pour out on the house of David and the inhabitants of Jerusalem a spirit of grace and supplication. They will look on me, the one they have pierced, and they will mourn for him as one mourns for an only child, and grieve bitterly for him as one grieves for a firstborn son.... On that day a fountain will be opened to the house of David

Quotation Marks

"The staggering dimensions of this conflict can scarcely be conceived. The battlefield will stretch from Megiddo on the north (Zechariah 12:11; Revelation 16:16) to Edom on the south (Isaiah 34:5 – 6; 63:1), a distance of approximately two hundred miles. It will reach from the Mediterranean Sea on the west to the hills of Moab on the east, a distance of almost one hundred miles. The center of the entire area will be the city of Jerusalem (Zechariah 14:1 – 2). Into this area the multiplied millions of men will be crowded for the final holocaust. The kings with their armies will come from the north and the south, from the east and from the west. There will be an invasion from hell beneath. And entering the scene at the last moment will be an invasion from space. In the most dramatic sense this will be the 'valley of decision' for humanity (Joel 3:14) and the great winepress into which will be poured the fierceness of the wrath of almighty God (Revelation 19:15)."

Herman Hoyt, in *The End Times* (Chicago: Moody Press, 1969), 163

DAYS OF HORROR

The Bible refers to the last great war with several titles of judgment and catastrophe:

A day of vengeance	Isaiah 34:8
The winepress of God's anger	Isaiah 63:2; Joel 3:13; Revelation 14:19 – 20
The great and dreadful day of the Lord	Joel 2:31; Malachi 4:5
The harvest	Joel 3:13; Revelation 14:15 – 16
The great day of God Almighty	Revelation 16:14

and the inhabitants of Jerusalem, to cleanse them from sin and impurity. (Zechariah 12:10; 13:1)

This is the day the apostle Paul looked forward to when he said, "And so all Israel will be saved" (Romans 11:26; see Joel 2:28 – 32).

Israel's turning to Jesus as her true Messiah will also bring about the fulfillment of God's promise to make a new covenant with Israel. (Read about it in Ezekiel 36:24 – 28 and Jeremiah 31:31 – 34.) The days of Israel's spiritual blindness will be over. The person Israel rejected when he came the first time will be welcomed as Israel's Deliverer in his second coming.

Jesus will take his place as King over the whole earth, as he removes wickedness and ushers in a Kingdom of peace (Psalm 2:5 – 6; Isaiah 2:1 – 4; Daniel 7:14; Zechariah 14:9).

Points 2 Remember

- ☑ Armageddon will be the last great war in human history.

- ☑ The Antichrist will try to exterminate the Jews who are living in Israel.

- ☑ Jesus will return to earth in glory and power to destroy the Antichrist and the armies of the world.

What Happens after Armageddon?

Many students of Bible prophecy believe that a period of seventy-five days will elapse between Jesus' return in power to defeat the armies of the Antichrist and the official beginning of Jesus' thousand-year Kingdom on earth. They base this conviction on the last verses of the book of Daniel in the Old Testament. Daniel has already predicted that his people will suffer under the Antichrist for 1,260 days (three and a half years) — but then Daniel writes this:

> From the time that the daily sacrifice is abolished and the abomination that causes desolation is set up [in the middle of the Tribulation], there will be 1,290 days. Blessed is the one who waits for and reaches the end of the 1,335 days. (Daniel 12:11 – 12)

Several events will most likely take place during this seventy-five-day span:

- The remnants of the Antichrist's government will be removed from Jerusalem and the rest of the earth.
- The Jews who survive the seven-year Tribulation will be regathered in the land of Israel and will be judged by the Lord. Those who have believed in Jesus as Messiah will enter the Kingdom and enjoy its blessings. Those who refuse to believe will die (Ezekiel 20:34 – 38; 36:24 – 28; Amos 9:14 – 15; Matthew 24:31).
- The Gentiles (non-Jews) who survive the Tribulation will also be judged. God will send his angels throughout the earth to remove

---

RAPTURE VERSUS RETURN

How the Two Phases of Jesus' Second Coming Compare

Rapture	Return
Jesus comes in the air	Jesus comes to the earth
Jesus comes *for* his church	Jesus comes *with* his church
Not predicted in the Old Testament	Often predicted in the Old Testament
No signs; can be at any moment	Many signs to watch for
Believers only are directly affected	Israel and the nations are directly affected
Only Christians will see Jesus	The world will see Jesus
Tribulation begins	Kingdom Age begins

unbelievers. Gentiles who have believed in Jesus will enter the Kingdom (Matthew 25:31 – 46; 13:47 – 50).

- The bodies of those who believed in the true God during the Old Testament era will be resurrected. Their spirits (which have been in heaven) will be reunited with new, glorified bodies (Isaiah 26:19; Daniel 12:2). The bodies of people who have believed in Jesus since the time of Jesus' death and resurrection were raised to life at the rapture, seven years earlier.
- Followers of Jesus who died during the Tribulation will also be resurrected (Revelation 20:4 – 6).

The War to End War

The key point to keep in mind as you think about Armageddon is that it is *God's* war. He is the one in control. He will move the plans and ambitions of future world leaders to bring them together at the right place and time. Human beings on their own will not bring history to an end. The end will come in God's time.

Great battles have echoed throughout history for hundreds of years — Bunker Hill, the Alamo, Gettysburg, Little Big Horn, Iwo Jima, the siege of Stalingrad, Operation Desert Storm — but these battles will sink into oblivion when Armageddon comes. The greatest armies ever assembled will be crushed by one word, one breath, from Jesus Christ.

DiGGiNG DeEpeR

✗ Ryrie, Charles. "The Campaign of Armageddon." In *Countdown to Armageddon.* Edited by Charles Ryrie. Eugene, Ore.: Harvest House, 1999, 196 – 207.

✗ Ice, Thomas, and Timothy Demy. *The Truth about Armageddon and the Middle East.* Eugene, Ore.: Harvest House, 1997.

HELP FILE

WARS AND RUMORS OF WARS

Jesus warned that the entire Tribulation would be marked by war and the threat of war (Matthew 24:6). As the apostle John began to see future events unfolded, a rider on a red horse sweeps throughout the world and takes peace from the earth (Revelation 6:4). Millions of people die as regional wars lead to famine and disease (Revelation 6:8).

The Bible also talks about other future wars — some on earth and some in heaven:

The Antichrist and the Enemy from the North

- Time: middle of the Tribulation
- Place: the land of Israel

Ezekiel 38 and 39 record a future invasion of the land of Israel by an enemy from the far north. The enemy is from the land of Magog, and their ruler is called Gog. ("Gog from Magog" — drop that into your conversation around the coffee machine tomorrow at work!) The leader of this northern army is said to be the prince of Rosh, Meshech, and Tubal (Ezekiel 38:1 – 2 NASB). Prophecy buffs have tried for years to equate Rosh with Russia and Meshech with Moscow. The words don't match, but geography does. The only foe far north of Israel capable of such a massive invasion is Russia. Moscow is straight north of Jerusalem.

These northern forces will have allies closer to Israel — Persia (modern Iran), Cush, and Put (countries south and west of Egypt, such as Sudan or Libya; Ezekiel 38:5 – 6). They will invade at a time when Israel seems to be at peace. This fits precisely with Israel's condition during the first half of the Tribulation. Israel will feel secure because she has a treaty with the powerful western ruler we know as the Antichrist.

Daniel in his prophetic writings talks about the same conflict but makes it clear that the Antichrist will get involved in the war as Israel's defender (Daniel 11:40 – 43). The northern enemy and her allies will march toward Israel, only to be met by a combination of the Antichrist's defensive army and the powerful judgment of God. God, for his own purposes, actually helps the Antichrist out!

It's possible that the Antichrist suffers a fatal wound during this war. Miraculously he survives this wound and rises up to defeat Gog and his allies. It will take Israel seven months to bury the dead and cleanse the land (Ezekiel 39:11 – 16). The vast expanse of Russia will be added to the Antichrist's empire.

Unfortunately (at least for Israel), the Antichrist will use his defense of Israel to betray the Jewish people. He will destroy the armies of Magog and then turn his own armies against Israel. He will claim the land of Israel as his own. Then the Antichrist will enter the rebuilt Temple in Jerusalem and proclaim himself to be god. Roman emperors had been declared gods by a powerless Roman senate; this future Roman emperor will decree *himself* to be god.

The Antichrist's Destruction of the False Church

- Time: middle of the Tribulation
- Place: worldwide

In the first three and a half years of the Tribulation, an apostate (think "false, unacceptable, departing from the truth") religious movement will arise throughout the western world under the blessing of the Antichrist. God's true church has been taken out of the world at the rapture. Genuine believers in Jesus will be driven into hiding during the Tribulation. But religion will flourish! The

remnants of unbelieving Christianity will merge with Islam and other world religions to produce a mixture of beliefs (and non-beliefs) acceptable to a world that hates and rejects the true God. This false church will support the Antichrist and be elevated to a place of great wealth and power. In Revelation, John sees this false religious system as a prostitute, dressed in fine clothes and covered with jewelry, riding atop the Antichrist in splendor (Revelation 17:1 – 6).

When the Antichrist announces himself to be god, however, even the false church will be shocked. The Antichrist will no longer need the apostate religious structure, so he will destroy it: "The beast and the ten horns you saw will hate the prostitute. They will bring her to ruin and leave her naked; they will eat her flesh and burn her with fire" (Revelation 17:16).

War between God's Angels and Satan

- Time: middle of the Tribulation
- Place: God's heaven

Tribulation battles are not limited to the

"Rather than being devoid of religion, the tribulation period will be one of the most religious periods of world history. [First] it will be a time of worldwide revival. Possibly the latter rain of the Spirit will be even more potent than the former rain of the Spirit at Pentecost. But though there will be many who will be saved and become followers of Jesus, there will also arise during the tribulation a great apostate church. At first the apostate church will be an ally of the Antichrist. . . . But when [the Antichrist] decrees himself god, he will tolerate no opposition."

Walter K. Price, in *The Coming Antichrist* (Chicago: Moody Press, 1974), 178, 180

MICHAEL THE ARCHANGEL

God has created millions of angels to carry out his will, but only two of them are named in the Bible. Gabriel (whose name means "Mighty One of God") is God's primary messenger angel. He is the one who brings important information to key players in the biblical drama. Michael (whose name means "Who Is Like God?") is the leader of God's heavenly army and is usually portrayed as the defender of God's people. Michael is called "one of the chief princes" of the angels in Daniel 10:13 and "the archangel" (highest angel) in Jude 9.

Michael plays a prominent role at two crucial points in the unfolding of God's future plan.

First, Michael protects the people of Israel who flee the Antichrist into the desert (Daniel 12:1). These Jews are sustained and hidden for the last three and a half years of the Tribulation in the area south of Jerusalem. Second, Michael leads the armies of heaven against Satan and the evil angels in the middle of the Tribulation (Revelation 12:7 – 9). Satan is cast out of heaven and confined to the earth.

References to Michael: Daniel 10:13, 21; 12:1; Jude 9; Revelation 12:7

References to Gabriel: Daniel 8:15 – 22; 9:21; Luke 1:19, 26

earth! In the middle of the Tribulation, God's holy angels, led by a powerful angel named Michael, fight against Satan and his angels. Some Christians believe that this battle took place long ago — before the creation of the world. Other Christians think that this is a summary of what took place in heaven when Jesus died on the cross and rose from the dead. But John places this event right at the midpoint of the seven-year Tribulation.

Contrary to what many people believe, Satan does not live in hell. Satan hates hell! Satan dwells today in the realm of our earth, but he has access to heaven — and he spends a lot of time there! In the Old Testament book of Job, God calls Satan in for regular reports (Job 1 – 2). John in Revelation says that Satan accuses Christians "before

our God day and night" (Revelation 12:10).

What happens in this midtribulation battle is that Satan and his angels are denied any further access to heaven and are confined to the earth. When Satan sees that he has only a short time before God's judgment falls, he turns his rage against Israel and against those who have come to believe in Jesus during the Tribulation. The Antichrist, Satan's instrument on earth, intensifies his persecution. A remnant of Israel is protected in the desert by God for the final three and a half years of the Tribulation, but most followers of Jesus are found and killed by the Antichrist. (The whole story of this heavenly battle and its aftermath can be read in Revelation 12:1 – 17.)

HELP FILE

IS AMERICA IN BIBLICAL PROPHECY?

America is never mentioned by name in the Bible — but other modern nations aren't either! Some students of prophecy, however, believe that the Bible indirectly identifies the United States in three passages.

The first is Ezekiel 38:13: "Sheba and Dedan and the merchants of Tarshish and all her villages will say to you [that is, to an army invading Israel in the Tribulation], 'Have you come to plunder? Have you gathered your hordes to loot?' " Tarshish was the farthest western point in the ancient world (modern Spain today). Some interpreters see this as a veiled reference to nations to the far west of Israel, including the United States.

A second passage is Revelation 12:14. When the Antichrist takes control of the Temple in Jerusalem, people from Israel (pictured as a woman in the passage) flee into the desert: "The woman was given the two wings of a great eagle, so that she might fly to the place prepared for her in the desert."

"The two wings of a great eagle" have been taken by some to mean a rescue airlift by the United States Air Force! It's true that in the modern world the eagle is the symbol of the United States (and to think that Ben-

jamin Franklin wanted the wild turkey to be our national bird!), but I can't imagine that John had the United States in mind when he wrote this. John used the wings of a great eagle to picture the swiftness and silence of their escape into the desert.

The third passage is Revelation 17 – 18, where the destruction of a great commercial center is described. Some interpreters believe the future "Babylon" will be New York City. After the terrorist attack on the twin towers of the World Trade Center in September 2001, many prophecy buffs were quoting these eerie, descriptive words:

Therefore in one day her plagues
    will overtake her:
  death, mourning and famine.
She will be consumed by fire,
    for mighty is the Lord God who
      judges her.

When the kings of the earth who committed adultery with her and shared her luxury see the smoke of her burning, they will weep and mourn over her. Terrified at her torment, they will stand far off and cry:

"Woe! Woe, O great city,
  O Babylon, city of power!
In one hour your doom has come!"

Revelation 18:8 – 10

My own opinion is that none of these passages refer directly to America. I think the United States will be part of the Antichrist's alliance. His base of power will be the old Roman Empire (western Europe) *and* those nations that trace their cultural and historical roots primarily to western Europe.

CHAPTER 7

Thy Kingdom Come: The Millennium

Thy Kingdom Come: The Millennium

Heads Up

▸ Take note, rulers of the world. A greater King is coming!

▸ Examine the "great debate" over the Kingdom of God

▸ Learn to live each day as a loyal subject of King Jesus

Okay, by now you know that Christians disagree on just about every aspect of end-times prophecy. The mother of all controversies, however, is the debate over the Kingdom. Endless rows of long, boring books have been written on exactly when Christ's Kingdom begins, what it is like, who is included, when it will end, if we are in it now or if we have to wait a while. It's enough to make you want to avoid the topic completely. But don't do it! Don't skip to another chapter! The Kingdom is an important biblical promise, and we really need to work at understanding it. And who knows — maybe when we really understand all the views on the Kingdom, we'll find ourselves closer to agreement than we thought possible.

As I've done with other controversial issues, I'll attempt to explain and explore each position. I'll give you the pros and cons for each, so you can do some serious thinking about where you stand. I may not change your position, but at least I'll make you aware of how other Christians see things.

Jesus Rules!

On two points we all agree! First, Christians believe that *Jesus Christ will one day return* to this world as the Judge of all humanity. He will return visibly and physically in power and majesty.

The second point we all agree on is that *Jesus Christ is the King*. He is the top, the pinnacle, the anointed ruler of the universe. No one and nothing are outside his control and care. We agree on that point because the Bible says it so clearly and so often. Let me give you a few samples of its kingly declarations:

The LORD is King for ever and ever. (Psalm 10:16)

The LORD is the true God;
　he is the living God, the eternal King. (Jeremiah 10:10)

Yours, O LORD, is the greatness and the power
　and the glory and the majesty and the splendor,
　for everything in heaven and earth is yours.
Yours, O LORD, is the kingdom;
　you are exalted as head over all.
Wealth and honor come from you;
　you are the ruler of all things. (1 Chronicles 29:11 – 12)

… God, the blessed and only Ruler, the King of kings and Lord of
　lords … (1 Timothy 6:15)

I saw heaven standing open and there before me was a white horse, whose rider is called Faithful and True.... On his robe and on his thigh he has this name written:

KING OF KINGS AND LORD OF LORDS. (Revelation 19:11, 16)

God reigns as King. God the Father has placed all authority and power in his Son, Jesus. So, more accurately, God the *Son,* Jesus Christ, reigns as King. He has always been the King, and he will always remain the King. No military coup will overthrow him. Death or incompetence won't remove him. Jesus rules!

And he rules over a Kingdom even now. Everything that exists falls under his authority. Listen to the Bible again:

Your kingdom is an everlasting kingdom,
　and your dominion endures through all generations. (Psalm 145:13)

The LORD has established his throne in heaven,
　and his kingdom rules over all. (Psalm 103:19)

[God] raised [Jesus] from the dead and seated him at his right hand, in the heavenly realms, far above all rule and authority, power and dominion, and every title that can be given, not only in the present age but also in the one to come. And God placed all things under his feet. (Ephesians 1:20 – 22)

You may not be convinced that Jesus is King over all when you read the headlines or hear the daily news reports of violence and war. That's why we need to read more than just the newspaper. God does reign, but he is allowing an evil world to run its course. Humanity's rebellion against God will ultimately bring human society to a crashing end. But even in the face of human rebellion against God's truth, God is in control. He is working all things together to accomplish exactly what he desires.

So — if Jesus reigns and if he already reigns over a Kingdom — what's the problem? Why are Christians still debating about the Kingdom of God? The debate arises from other passages of Scripture that picture the Kingdom of God as the visible reign of Jesus on earth. God's great King will rule over a Kingdom of peace and prosperity. Even Jesus taught his followers to pray that God's Kingdom would come (Matthew 6:10). The Bible passage quoted in every discussion of the Kingdom is Revelation 20:1 – 6:

> And I saw an angel coming down out of heaven, having the key to the Abyss and holding in his hand a great chain. He seized the dragon, that ancient serpent, who is the devil, or Satan, and bound him for a thousand years. He threw him into the Abyss, and locked and sealed it over him, to keep him from deceiving the nations anymore until the thousand years were ended. After that, he must be set free for a short time.
>
> I saw thrones on which were seated those who had been given authority to judge. And I saw the souls of those who had been beheaded because of their testimony for Jesus and because of the word of God. They had not worshiped the beast or his image and had not received his mark on their foreheads or their hands. They came to life and reigned with Christ a thousand years. (The rest of the dead did not come to life until the thousand years were ended.) This is the first resurrection. Blessed and holy are those who have part in the first resurrection. The second death has no power over them, but they will be priests of God and of Christ and will reign with him for a thousand years.

Here's the question: When will we "reign with him for a thousand years"? When will we see that visible Kingdom come — or can we see it today if we look in the right places? That's the heart of the big debate — what does the promised Kingdom of God look like and when will it come?

Christians have given three basic answers to these questions. The advocates of each position believe that the Bible promises a Kingdom. The division comes with respect to *when the Kingdom comes* in the plan of God. Each of the three views on the Kingdom are "millennial" views — that is, they focus on the promised one-thousand-year (= millennium) reign of Jesus Christ.

View #1 of the Kingdom: "We're in It Today!"

Christians who hold this view of the Kingdom of God call themselves *amillennialists*. Putting the letter "a" in front of the word "millennium" makes it mean "no millennium." Simply stated, they believe that there will be no *future* thousand-year reign of Christ on earth. Instead, Christ reigns right now in heaven and in his church on earth. We are in Christ's Kingdom today.

In the Spotlight: Presenting the Case for the Amillennial Position

Amillennialists base their position on the following arguments:

- Jesus could return at any time. When he returns, Jesus will bring human history to an end in one big bang. Jesus will come to earth, all human beings who ever lived will be resurrected (their bodies raised back to life), every person will be judged by God, and each will be sent to his or her eternal destiny. There will be no thousand-year

Amillennialism

To say that amillennialists believe in *no* millennium is really not accurate. They believe in a Kingdom reign of Christ but are convinced that we are living in the Kingdom right now. They do not accept a *future* earthly reign of Christ.

Techno-Speak

Kingdom on earth. The "rapture" of Christians and the "return" of Jesus to the earth in power and majesty are one climactic event.

- The "one thousand years" of Christ's reign mentioned in Revelation 20 is to be understood as a symbolic number, not a literal number. Nowhere else in the Bible is one thousand years mentioned as the length of the Kingdom. John was using a large, round number to convey the idea of "a long time" to his readers. He did not expect them to take it literally.

- God did make promises to Israel in the Old Testament about an earthly Kingdom of peace and prosperity. When Israel rejected Jesus as their Messiah, however, God transferred those promises to the Christian community — the church, the *new* Israel. All God's promises are being fulfilled spiritually today. Christians enjoy the spiritual blessings of God's Kingdom. We will also see a literal fulfillment of the Bible's promises in God's *eternal* Kingdom on a new earth.

- Satan has been "bound" in this age, just as Revelation 20:1 – 3 predicted. This doesn't mean that Satan is inactive. He still opposes the work of God, but he can no longer deceive the nations. Before Jesus' death and resurrection, all the nations and cultures of the world (except for the people of Israel) were in darkness and under Satan's dominion. Only Israel possessed the truth of God. Because of Jesus' victory over Satan on the cross, the gospel message is now made available to the entire world. Satan can no longer prevent the spread of God's truth to every nation. Near the end of the present gospel age, Satan will be loosed for a short time, and he will deceive the nations again to fight against the Lord and his people (Revelation 20:7 – 10). God will destroy those who come against God's people, and Satan will be confined to an eternal lake of fire.

- Jesus made it clear throughout his ministry that the Kingdom of God was "near" (Matthew 4:17) and that some of his own disciples would "not taste death before they see the Son of Man coming in his kingdom" (Matthew 16:28). Was Jesus mistaken, or did the Kingdom actually begin on the day of Pentecost when the Holy Spirit began to form the Christian community — the church? The Kingdom can't be "near" if we've waited almost two thousand years to see it.

- Many of Jesus' parables picture the Kingdom as the time *between* Jesus' first coming and his second coming, not as a time *after* his second coming. The Kingdom is compared to a field where good

MAJOR PLAYERS

The amillennial view of God's Kingdom is held by the Roman Catholic Church, Eastern Orthodox churches, and many Protestants. The foundations of this view are usually traced back to Augustine, a fifth-century church leader and teacher (A.D. 354 – 430). The Protestant reformers John Calvin and Martin Luther also taught an amillennial view.

grain and weeds grow up together until the final judgment at the end (Matthew 13:24 – 29, 36 – 43). In the two thousand years since Jesus' first coming, the field of the world has been populated both by those who follow Jesus and those who don't believe. In a final climactic judgment, Jesus will separate "the wheat" from "the weeds." (See also Jesus' parables of the mustard seed [Matthew 13:31 – 32] and the fishing net [Matthew 13:47 – 50].)

- Those who expect a visible Kingdom on earth have missed what Paul said in Romans 14:17: "For the kingdom of God is not a matter of eating and drinking [literal activities], but of righteousness, peace and joy in the Holy Spirit [spiritual qualities]." Jesus reigns over his Kingdom right now. He reigns in heaven over the spirits of Christians who have died, and he reigns on earth in his church and in the hearts of Christians.

- Plenty of verses in the New Testament say that God's Kingdom is *now* and that Christians are in it right now. Two samples: "I declare to you, brothers, that flesh and blood cannot inherit the kingdom of God, nor does the perishable inherit the imperishable" (1 Corinthians 15:50). That is to say, the Kingdom isn't physical (as in a future, thousand-year, visible reign on earth); the Kingdom is spiritual (as in Christ's reign in our hearts). The apostle Paul also said that when a person believes in Jesus, the person is rescued from Satan's dominion and brought into the Kingdom of Christ (Colossians 1:13). So we are in the Kingdom now. The only kingdom Paul looked for beyond the present Kingdom was God's "heavenly kingdom" (2 Timothy 4:18).

- The book of Revelation does not describe a series of events that happen one after the other. Instead, the book is composed of sections that run parallel to each other and that each portrays the church and the world in this present age. Therefore, just because John's description of the Kingdom in Revelation 20 was written after his account of Jesus' return to earth in Revelation 19, it does *not* mean that the Kingdom becomes a reality after Jesus' return. John, as he has done several times already in Revelation, simply backs up and describes the present age from a different perspective.

- When John sees faithful Christians seated on thrones and reigning with Christ for a thousand years (Revelation 20:4 – 6), he is referring to Christians reigning *in heaven* right now with Christ, not to Christians reigning over a future earthly Kingdom.

Under the Searchlight: An Evaluation of the Amillennial Position

There are some really good things to say about the amillennial position. Christians who hold this position have tried to deal with what the Bible says and, at the same time, keep things simple and straightforward. They have not become bogged down in endless controversies over minor details of biblical prophecy. Amillennialists have tried to take the nature of biblical literature seriously. They recognize that prophecy contains a lot of symbolism — and they have tried to handle that symbolism consistently.

An honest evaluation of the amillennial view, however, raises some serious questions. The main issues center on Revelation 20.

AN AMILLENNIALIST EXPLAINS

"There is no indication in these verses [Revelation 20:1 – 6] that John is describing an earthly millennial reign. The scene is set in heaven. Nothing is said in verses 4 – 6 about the earth, about Palestine as the center of this reign, about the Jews. Nothing is said here about believers who are still on earth during this millennial reign — the vision deals exclusively with believers who have died. This millennial reign is not something to be looked for in the future; it is going on now, and will be until Christ returns. Hence the term <u>realized millennium</u> is an apt description of the view — if it is remembered that the millennium in question is not an earthly but a heavenly reign."

Anthony Hoekema, in *The Bible and the Future*
(Grand Rapids: Eerdmans, 1979), 235

- Six times in Revelation 20:1 – 6 we read the term "one thousand years." How can we simply decide to call that a "symbolic" number and make it refer to "a long time"? It's true that the Bible doesn't refer anywhere else to Christ's Kingdom as lasting a thousand years, but how many times does the Bible have to say it for it to be true? Amillennialists even admit that if a person reads the passage in Revelation 20 "literally," this person is forced to accept a future millennial reign of Christ on earth.

- John clearly places the thousand-year reign of Christ *after* the return of Christ to earth in visible glory. To suggest that John backs up at the beginning of Revelation 20 and reviews the Church Age again is an interpretation imposed on the text of the Bible, not one drawn from the text. If you just read the book of Revelation, you would conclude that John is talking about a thousand-year period of time after Jesus returns to the earth.

- Revelation 20:1 – 3 pictures Satan's "binding" as his removal from the earth. He is confined to the Abyss, a spiritual prison. This is certainly not Satan's condition in our present age. Paul and other New Testament writers portray Satan as actively engaged in opposition to God, God's people, and the gospel message. To say that Satan is "bound" only in the sense that he cannot hinder the spread of the gospel does not do justice to what the Bible says. Jesus triumphantly defeated Satan through Jesus' death on the cross and his resurrection, but this victory will only be finalized when Satan is thrown into the lake of fire.

- There is certainly a sense in which we see aspects of the Kingdom functioning today. Christians know what it means to have Christ ruling as Lord in their hearts, and Christ unquestionably reigns supreme in heaven as God's exalted Son. But amillennialists only look at part of the biblical information about the Kingdom. What about the promises in the Old Testament to Israel of a glorious Kingdom of peace and prosperity — promises that have yet to be fulfilled? What about the references in the New Testament to our future entrance into the Kingdom? (Check out 2 Peter 1:10 – 11.)

- Revelation 20:4 – 5 pictures two resurrections separated by a thousand years of time: "I saw the souls of those who had been beheaded because of their testimony for Jesus.... They came to life and reigned with Christ a thousand years. (The rest of the dead did not come to life until the thousand years were ended.)" How else can

THE FUTURE THROUGH AN AMILLENNIAL TELESCOPE

A parallel growth of both good (God's Kingdom)
and evil (Satan's Kingdom) in this present age

Jesus returns to earth in visible glory

The resurrection of all people

The judgment of all people

Eternity

that be interpreted except that the followers of Christ are raised to life and reign with Christ over a thousand-year Kingdom, and then, a thousand years later, the rest of the dead (that is, unbelievers) are raised to face God's judgment? Amillennialists have to say that those who die for the cause of Christ "came to life" in a spiritual sense in heaven, and they reign with Christ in heaven. Then when Christ returns to earth at the end of the Church-Age Kingdom, *all* the dead are raised to life physically to face God's judgment. Quite a stretch! It seems clear that "came to life" means a bodily resurrection both times it is used in the passage. Because this is the case, one group must be resurrected at the beginning of the thousand years, and the other group at the end.

DiGGinG DeEpeR

If you want to read an excellent presentation of the amillennial view of prophecy, pick up

✗ Hoekema, Anthony. *The Bible and the Future*. Grand Rapids: Eerdmans, 1979.

✗ Butler, Paul. *Approaching the New Millennium: An Amillennial Look at* A.D. *2000*. Joplin, Mo.: College Press, 1998.

A classic amillennial commentary on the book of Revelation is

✗ Hendriksen, William. *More Than Conquerors*. Grand Rapids: Baker, 1940 and many reprints.

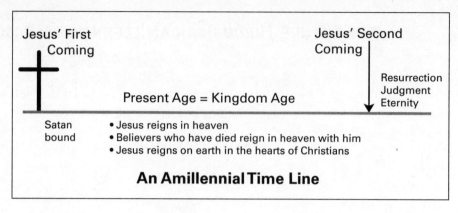

An Amillennial Time Line

- The Bible's descriptions of the peace and prosperity of the earthly Kingdom are also accurate descriptions of our eternal home on a newly created earth. But it doesn't mean that there will be no earthly Kingdom. Christ's earthly millennial reign will merge into his eternal reign.

View #2 of the Kingdom: "We're Moving toward It!"

A second view of God's Kingdom is *post*millennialism — the belief that Jesus will return to earth *after* a long golden age in which the Christian faith is embraced by virtually the entire world. Simply stated, postmils believe that the gospel message will continue to advance its way throughout the world. Ultimately every nation and ethnic group will believe in Jesus as Savior and Lord and will seek to follow biblical principles. This universal embrace of Jesus will usher in an unprecedented age of prosperity and peace — a millennial paradise. At the end of the future age of peace, Jesus will return to earth and eternity will begin.

In the Spotlight: The Postmillennial Position

- The millennium that postmillennialists look for is a golden age of spiritual and material prosperity. It will be brought about by forces already at work in our world. As more and more individuals believe in Christ, the social, moral, economic, political, and cultural life of the nations of the world will gradually be conformed to Christian principles until the entire world is "Christianized." The peace and spiritual blessing that Christians experience now in their own hearts and occasionally in Christian families or in Christian churches will spread to the entire community and world. This doesn't mean that eventually every single person will become a Christian or that all evil will be gone from human society. It means that evil will be reduced to almost nothing and that Christian principles will guide society as a whole.

- This hope of a virtually universal salvation was anticipated even in the Old Testament:

> Turn to me and be saved,
>   all you ends of the earth;
>   for I am God, and there is no other.
> By myself I have sworn,
>   my mouth has uttered in all integrity
>   a word that will not be revoked:
> Before me every knee will bow;
>   by me every tongue will swear. (Isaiah 45:22 – 23)

- Jesus did not picture the Kingdom coming to earth suddenly. He pictured it as a growing influence, gradually increasing in size and power. The Kingdom will grow like a mustard seed until it fills the earth (Luke 13:18 – 19). It will work its way through society as yeast works its way through bread dough — silently and gradually (Luke 13:20 – 21).
- Postmillennialists base their view of the ultimate conversion of the world on Jesus' command in Matthew 28:18 – 20:

> Then Jesus came to them and said, "All authority in heaven and on earth has been given to me. Therefore go and make disciples of all nations, baptizing them in the name of the Father and of the Son and of the Holy Spirit, and teaching them to obey everything I have commanded you. And surely I am with you always, to the very end of the age."

- Jesus' intention was that Christians would courageously do what he told them to do. Jesus even guaranteed their final victory. Those who hold this view of the Kingdom admit that Christians haven't done a very effective job of evangelizing the world in the two thousand years since Jesus went back to heaven. But in time the message of the gospel will succeed in accomplishing what Jesus intended. Even the gates of hell will not be able to withstand the steady advance of the Christian faith (Matthew 16:18). Jesus even predicted the worldwide proclamation of the gospel before this age would end: "And this gospel of the kingdom will be preached in the whole world as a testimony to all nations, and then the end will come" (Matthew 24:14). Jesus is not an *absent* King who will do great things when he returns; he is a *present* King who has given his full authority to the Christian community.

- This present age will gradually merge into a millennial age as an increasing percentage of the world's inhabitants are converted to Christianity. The Kingdom of God is visible today in Christ's reign in our hearts, but the day is coming when our entire social, political, and economic structures will reflect Christ's lordship.

- The millennial age will continue at least one thousand years or even longer. It will conclude with Jesus' visible return to earth, the resurrection and judgment of all human beings, and the ushering in of eternity.

- Progress in health care, technology, education, travel, and communications, as well as economic advance and political freedom, can all

A POSTMILLENNIALIST EXPLAINS

Quotation Marks

"Postmillennialism is that view of the last things which holds that the kingdom of God is now being extended in the world through the preaching of the gospel and the saving work of the Holy Spirit in the hearts of individuals, that the world eventually is to be Christianized, and that the return of Christ is to occur at the close of a long period of righteousness and peace commonly called the millennium. . . .

"The millennium to which the postmillennialist looks forward is thus a golden age of spiritual prosperity during this present dispensation, that is, the Church Age. This is to be brought about through forces now active in the world. It is to last an indefinitely long period of time, perhaps much longer than a literal one thousand years. The changed character of individuals will be reflected in an uplifted social, economic, political, and cultural life of mankind."

Loraine Boettner, in *The Meaning of the Millennium: Four Views*, ed. Robert Clouse (Downers Grove, Ill: InterVarsity Press, 1977), 117

be directly or indirectly traced to the influence of Christian ideals in human society.

- Postmillennialists interpret biblical prophecy as nonliteral and spiritual. Their contention is that the Jews of Jesus' day were literalists who looked for an earthly, political Messiah, and as a result they missed what God was actually doing. First-century Jews rejected the true Messiah because Jesus came with an invitation into a *spiritual* Kingdom. Christians who are literalists when it comes to biblical prophecy may miss what God is actually doing as they look for so-called "signs of the end times." Instead of worrying about the Antichrist, we should be focusing on confidently declaring the gospel message and advancing God's Kingdom on earth.

Under the Searchlight: An Evaluation of Postmillennialism

Postmillennialists have made some very positive contributions to the Christian worldview. For one thing, postmillennialists have not been satisfied with a weak, stumbling proclamation of the gospel message. They have pushed Christians to recognize that all of Jesus' authority stands behind the message. We don't have to feel embarrassed to tell someone about Jesus and his salvation! Our lifestyle should be courageously focused on Jesus.

Postmillennialists have also promoted an optimistic view of the future of human society. Some Christians who hold other millennial positions tend to think that the world will get worse and worse, and so they throw up their hands in despair and retreat into the safety of their church buildings. Postmillennialists encourage all of us to be actively pursuing justice and peace and racial equality and economic opportunity.

The postmillennialists have a lot of very positive things to say about the future. But is it what the Bible teaches? Christians who have taken a serious look at the postmil position have raised some tough questions:

- No Christian questions the urgency of Jesus' final command to his disciples to carry the gospel message to the ends of the earth. But while Jesus assured them of his authority and presence, he did not promise anything like universal reception of the gospel. Jesus regularly made it clear that only some of those who heard the truth would respond in faith. The gate to life, Jesus said, was narrow — and only a few would find it (Matthew 7:14). The majority of human beings would choose the road to destruction. Most people would, in fact, choose spiritual darkness over spiritual light (John 3:19). In the story Jesus told of a man sowing seeds of grain, only one seed out of four found fertile ground and produced fruit (Mark 4:3 – 20). The Word of God is to be proclaimed to every person, but not every person will respond in acceptance.

- There is no evidence that Jesus or any of the New Testament writers looked forward to universal reception of the gospel in this age before Jesus' return to earth. This age will be marked by tribulation and persecution for Christians. Sweeping revival has at times come to certain nations, and Christians energetically pray for spiritual renewal today — but the Bible never promises a truly Christianized world.

- The Bible often pictures the Kingdom of God coming suddenly, not gradually. God's reign sweeps away the human governments of the world in one blow. The Old Testament prophet Daniel saw a great image representing successive human empires. Then a great

THE FUTURE THROUGH A POSTMILLENNIAL TELESCOPE

Progressive advance of the gospel and improvement in social and economic conditions

Eventually the world is Christianized and a long period of peace and prosperity follows

Jesus returns to earth at the end of the golden age

The resurrection of all people

The judgment of all people

Eternity

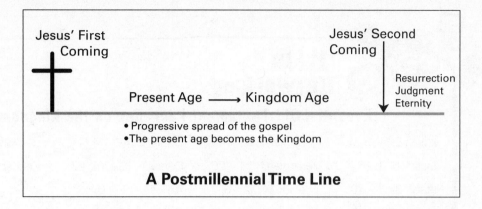

A Postmillennial Time Line

stone flew from heaven and smashed the statue and filled the earth (Daniel 2:34 – 35, 44 – 45). The visible Kingdom of God will not be brought in by the diligent effort of evangelizing Christians, but by the powerful return of God's King.

- When the Bible pictures the Kingdom growing gradually, it also at times pictures evil growing right with it. In Jesus' parable of the wheat and the weeds, the weeds (representing evil) were allowed to grow along with the good grain (representing the followers of Jesus). The weeds were not transformed into good grain. They grew to maturity and then were separated out at the end of the age (Matthew 13:24 – 30). Doesn't that picture contradict the idea of a more and more Christianized world?

- Several passages of Scripture teach that morality *will* get worse and worse as the present age nears its end. (Check out Matthew 24:9 – 14; Luke 17:26 – 30; 2 Timothy 3:1 – 5.) There is a sense in which the world is improving — but there is also a sense in which the moral and spiritual climate is getting worse. We certainly can't ignore the spread of the Christian faith in areas of Africa and South America or the easing of oppression toward Christians in Russia and eastern Europe. But those positive leaps are counterbalanced by declining morality in western nations and the rise of violence worldwide. The weakening of moral values is happening in spite of the church's presence and influence. The only real hope for permanent positive change in human society is the personal return of Jesus to establish a Kingdom of righteousness and peace and justice.

Bible NetWorking

Essential Old Testament Passages on the Kingdom

Isaiah 2:1 – 5	Jeremiah 31:1 – 40	Daniel 2:44	Zechariah 12:6 – 10
Isaiah 11:1 – 6	Jeremiah 33:1 – 26	Daniel 7:13 – 14, 27	Zechariah 14:6 – 2
Isaiah 32:1 – 20	Ezekiel 34:22 – 31	Amos 9:11 – 15	
Isaiah 35:1 – 10	Ezekiel 36:24 – 30	Zechariah 2:10 – 13	
Isaiah 60:1 – 22	Ezekiel 37:20 – 28	Zechariah 6:11 – 13	

- Jesus said in Luke 18:8, "When the Son of Man comes, will he find faith on the earth?" This question suggests that when Jesus returns, the number of genuine believers will be small, and yet postmillennialists say that Jesus will return to a virtually Christian world.

View #3 of the Kingdom: "Jesus Will Bring It!"

The *premillennial* view of the Kingdom holds that Jesus will return visibly to earth *before* the Kingdom Age. Premillennialists believe that the Kingdom of God will be a literal, earthly Kingdom of one thousand years during which Jesus will reign over the earth from Jerusalem. The Kingdom will arrive suddenly and powerfully when Jesus returns from heaven and destroys his enemies. Satan will be removed from the earth for the period of the thousand-year Kingdom, and the effects of sin's curse will be lifted. Believers from the Old Testament and Christians from the present age will be resurrected and will reign with Jesus over the earth.

Most premillennialists would agree with amils and postmils that Jesus rules over his church in this age and that he rules in the hearts of his people. They would make it clear, however, that Jesus' reign today is not to be confused with the future Kingdom when Jesus will rule on earth as King for a thousand years.

In the Spotlight: The Premillennial Position

Premillennialists base their position on the following evidence:

- Premillennialism is the only view that takes Revelation 20:1 – 6 at face value, namely, in its normal sense. Six times in this passage the Bible says that Christ will rule over a Kingdom that lasts one thousand years. Also in Revelation, John makes it clear that the Kingdom is established *after* Christ's return to earth in power and glory (Revelation 19:11 – 21).
- The premillennial view says that the two resurrections in Revelation 20:4 – 5 are just that — two separate bodily resurrections. Believers who have died in the Tribulation are raised to life at the beginning of the thousand years. They reign with Christ over the Kingdom. Then, one thousand years later, at the end of the Kingdom Age, "the rest of the dead" (that is, unbelievers) are raised to life to stand before God's final judgment (Revelation 20:11 – 15).
- Premils accept the fact that the Kingdom is said to be one thousand years in length only in Revelation 20. But they add that the *concept* of a visible Kingdom on this earth is taught throughout the Bible. God promised Abraham (the human father of the nation of Israel, the Jews) the land of Palestine as a permanent dwelling place (Genesis 12:1 – 3; 15:18 – 19). The Jews have held the land at various times for varying lengths of time, but never permanently. God also promised Israel's King David that his kingdom would last forever

MEET THE PLAYERS

The view that Jesus will return to reign over a thousand-year Kingdom was the view of the early church. Almost all the church leaders in the first three centuries after Jesus' resurrection held to a premillennial view. The fifth-century church leader, Augustine, was the one who suggested that the Kingdom of God was really a spiritual Kingdom made visible in the earthly church (the amillennial view). His view soon replaced premillennialism as the majority view. Premillennialism made a comeback in the middle of the nineteenth century and is currently a very widely held view of end-times events. Some well-known premillennialists are Charles Ryrie, John Walvoord, Hal Lindsey, Chuck Swindoll, and John MacArthur Jr. *The Scofield Reference Bible* and the *Ryrie Study Bible* are strongly premillennial in their interpretation of biblical prophecy.

and that one of David's descendants would sit on Israel's throne forever (2 Samuel 7:12 – 16; 1 Chronicles 28:5, 7). The prophet Isaiah announced the coming of a king who would reign over a kingdom without end (Isaiah 9:6 – 7). Daniel and Ezekiel and Zechariah echoed the same promises. The angel Gabriel told Mary that her son, Jesus, would sit on the throne of David and rule over Israel forever (Luke 1:32 – 33). The apostle Paul encouraged his friend Timothy to be faithful to the Lord in anticipation of the soon coming of Jesus and his Kingdom (2 Timothy 4:1).

- Jesus came the first time proclaiming that the Kingdom of God was near. He was not offering a *different* Kingdom from the one God had promised in the Old Testament but the *same* Kingdom. He was not offering a purely *spiritual* Kingdom (in the church) but also a political and social Kingdom based on allegiance to himself as King. Jesus offered himself to Israel as her promised King, but the people (as a whole) rejected Jesus and agreed to his death. That generation wanted the Kingdom, but they didn't want Jesus as King! God judged Israel for her rejection of Jesus in A.D. 70 when the Romans destroyed Jerusalem. Furthermore, God *postponed* the establishment of the visible Kingdom until Jesus' second coming. Christians

Techno-Speak

Dispensationalism

Some premillennialists also call themselves "dispensationalists," meaning they believe that God has dealt with his people in different ways throughout human history. The various eras of human history are called *dispensations* — thus the unusual name. Under the Law in the Old Testament, for example, God dealt with his people (Israel) according to certain household rules. Those rules changed when God moved to the present dispensation, the Church Age. The household rules will be altered again in the next dispensation, the Kingdom Age.

Dispensationalists do *not* believe that people have been saved in different ways. Human beings throughout all of history have been made right with God in only one way — by God's grace, through faith in God's promises. The *content* of God's promises changes from one dispensation to the next, but the *process* of salvation is always the same. Premillennialists who are not dispensationalists are called "historic premillennialists." (Try dropping *that* sentence at your next office meeting. They may let you leave early!)

enjoy some aspects of the Kingdom today, but the fullness of the Kingdom will only come when Jesus the King returns to the earth.

- Most premillennialists distinguish between *Israel* (the people descended from Abraham through his son Isaac and his grandson Jacob; the Jews) and the *church* (all individuals who have received Jesus as Savior and Lord). God focused his program in the Old Testament on Israel. When Israel rejected Jesus as her Messiah, God moved his focus to a worldwide outreach through the Christian community, the church. When Jesus returns to earth, he will focus once again on Israel and the fulfillment of God's Kingdom promises to her. The prophet Zechariah makes the point that the Jews will hold a place of prominence in the millennial Kingdom (Zechariah 8:23). Christians will also enjoy the benefits of the Kingdom, because we are co-heirs with Israel of all of God's promises (Ephesians 3:6). The church is *not* the new Israel. Israel is still Israel, and the church is the church.

- The promises of an *earthly* Kingdom cannot be generalized to refer to God's *eternal* Kingdom on a new earth. Kingdom promises are linked to specific places on this present earth — Mount Zion, Jerusalem, Egypt (Psalm 2:6; Zechariah 14:18 – 19). Nations of the earth will see this Kingdom (Psalm 2:7 – 9, 12; Isaiah 52:10; Daniel 7:14), and Jesus will carry out judgment on any who rebel (Ezekiel 20:33 – 38). There will be no rebellion in God's *eternal* Kingdom on a newly created earth.

- Premillennialists (well, *most* premillennialists) believe that a seven-year Tribulation will ravage the earth just before Jesus' visible return. The Tribulation will be a time of intense judgment from God. Human society will collapse under the weight of unrestrained evil and of God's devastating judgment. Premillennialists differ on whether Christians who are alive when the Tribulation begins will go through the Tribulation or be raptured out before the Tribulation.

- The future Kingdom will be a time of peace and prosperity — exactly what God, in his Old Testament promises, pictured the Kingdom to be. Think about these incredible benefits:

  ✗ War will disappear, and the industries of war will be focused on peaceful ends (Zechariah 9:10; Isaiah 2:4; 9:7).

  ✗ Social justice, moral purity, and racial harmony will permeate the fabric of human culture (Psalm 72:1 – 4, 12 – 14; Isaiah 42:3).

✘ Physical deformity and disease will be eradicated (Isaiah 33:24; 35:5 – 6; 61:1 – 2).

✘ Long life will be the norm (Isaiah 65:20 – 22).

✘ The earth will be abundantly productive (Psalm 72:16; Isaiah 35:1 – 2; Amos 9:13).

✘ Even wild animals will become nonthreatening (Isaiah 11:6 – 9; 65:25).

✘ The knowledge of the true God will extend to every person in every nation (Isaiah 66:23).

- The worship of God during the Millennium will center in the rebuilt Temple in Jerusalem (Isaiah 2:3; 60:13; Ezekiel 40 – 48; Joel 3:18; Haggai 2:7, 9). The Old Testament prophets make it clear that animal sacrifices will be reinstated in this millennial Temple too (Isaiah 56:6 – 7; 60:7; Ezekiel 43:18 – 27; 45:17 – 23; Zechariah 14:16 – 21). These sacrifices will not be offered to cover sin, as they were in the Old Testament. No animal sacrifice can ever take away sin anyway (Hebrews 10:1 – 2). The millennial sacrifices will instead be a memorial to the ultimate sacrifice of Jesus on the cross. They will serve as a reminder of the price that was required to bring salvation to the human race.

A PREMILLENNIALIST (OR TWO) EXPLAINS

Quotation Marks

"Premillennialism generally holds to a revival of the Jewish nation and their repossession of their ancient land when Christ returns. Satan will be bound and a kingdom of righteousness, peace, and tranquility will ensue. The righteous are raised from the dead before the millennium and participate in its blessings. The wicked dead are not raised until after the millennium."

John Walvoord, in *The Millennial Kingdom* (Grand Rapids: Zondervan, 1959), 5 – 6

"I and every other completely orthodox Christian feel certain that there will be a resurrection of the flesh, followed by one thousand years in the rebuilt, embellished, and enlarged city of Jerusalem, as was announced by the prophets Ezekiel, Isaiah, and others."

Justin Martyr (A.D. 100 – 165), an early Christian theologian, in *Dialogue with Trypho*, 80

A CHRISTMAS CAROL?

When Isaac Watts wrote the song "Joy to the World," he wasn't thinking about Christmas! He was writing about Jesus' second coming to reign as King over the earth. Think about the words:

Joy to the world! The Lord is come:
Let earth receive her King ...

No more let sins and sorrows grow,
Nor thorns infest the ground ...

He rules the world
    with truth and grace ...

This is a Millennium carol! It celebrates the time when Jesus will reign over a world of peace.

- At the end of the thousand-year reign of Christ, Satan will be loosed. He will incite those people who have outwardly submitted to Christ's rule but never truly believed in him as Savior. The rebellion will end with God's destruction of unbelievers and the confinement of Satan forever in the lake of fire (Revelation 20:7 – 10).
- Jesus' reign will be a "forever" reign because his reign over a *restored earth* in the Kingdom will be extended to his reign over a *new earth* for eternity. Only genuine believers in Jesus Christ will inhabit the new earth, our eternal heavenly home (Revelation 21:1 – 8).

Under the Searchlight: An Evaluation of Premillennialism

On the positive side, Christians who hold to the premillennial perspective have been far more serious about studying biblical prophecy than Christians who hold other views. Sometimes this interest becomes an obsession, but, all in all, premillennialists have tried to validate the Bible's strong emphasis on the future. Premillennialists have also tried to take the Bible's words seriously. Their concern for the literal interpretation of Scripture has motivated them to allow the Bible to speak for itself.

Christians of other persuasions aren't persuaded, however. They have looked closely at the premillennial position and have raised some interesting issues:

- Jesus spoke at length about future events on several occasions but never predicted a thousand-year earthly reign. When the apostle

THE FUTURE THROUGH A PREMILLENNIAL TELESCOPE

The rapture of Christians from the earth

Seven-year Tribulation on earth

The battle of Armageddon

Jesus returns to earth in power and majesty

The thousand-year reign of Jesus on the earth

The final judgment of unbelievers

Eternity

Paul talked about the second coming, he made no mention of Jesus establishing an earthly Kingdom. Maybe John's references in Revelation 20 to a thousand-year period *should* be taken in some way other than a literal millennial reign of Jesus on earth. In fact, why do we need an earthly millennium at all? Isn't it simpler to view Jesus' second coming as the climax of human history?

• God did make promises to Israel in the Old Testament about an earthly Kingdom, but those promises were always conditional. God warned Israel over and over that her disobedience would cancel the promises of future blessing. So we aren't looking for any more Old Testament promises to be fulfilled. The promises either have already been fulfilled (in Jesus' first coming, for example) or forfeited because of Israel's disobedience. God's promise to Abraham to give his descendants all the land of Palestine was fulfilled when Joshua conquered the land (Joshua 21:43, 45). The people of Israel lost the land because of their disobedience, not because God failed to keep his promise. David's sons did rule over Israel — until they forfeited their right to rule because of their own disobedience to the Lord. When Jesus came and the people rejected him, all the promises God made about the Messiah's reign were transferred to a *new* Israel, the church. Israel forfeited the Kingdom when they crucified the King!

• The Kingdom was entrusted to the church, the body of genuine believers in Jesus. Christians enjoy the *spiritual* blessings of the Kingdom now and the *complete* blessings of the Kingdom in an eternal home on a new earth.

- Premillennialists are so focused on the "literal" view of Scripture that they ignore its literary form and fail to see how much of biblical prophecy is figurative and symbolic. When John wrote the book of Revelation, he did not intend or expect that his readers would take the "one thousand years" in Revelation 20 in a wooden, literal sense. He used the phrase as a symbol to convey "a long time."

- Jesus said that the Kingdom of God was "near" and "at hand." Was Jesus mistaken — or misled? Why do we have to wait more than two thousand years for a Kingdom that is near? Jesus also told his disciples that some of them would not experience death until they saw the Kingdom of God come with power (Mark 9:1). The Kingdom began on the day of Pentecost in Acts 2 when the Holy Spirit came on the followers of Jesus with power (Acts 1:8; 2:1 – 4). The Kingdom exists in its fullness today. Jesus reigns in heaven on David's throne (Acts 2:29 – 32). Jesus reigns over his people. When we believe in Jesus, we are transferred into the Kingdom (Colossians 1:13). When Jesus comes again, it will not be to reign over a millennial Kingdom. He will come to bring human history to a close and usher in the *eternal* Kingdom of God.

- The Old Testament passages premillennialists quote as descriptive of the future Kingdom on earth are better understood in the context of the final eternal home of believers, the new earth created by God at the end of human history.

- Premillennialists want to make a clear distinction between Israel and the church, but the New Testament says that the division between believing Gentiles (non-Jews) and believing Jews has been broken down (Ephesians 2:14). Believing Gentiles belong to the

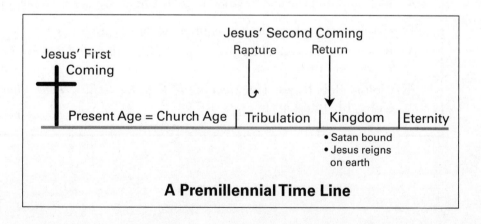

A Premillennial Time Line

same household of God to which believing Jews belong (Ephesians 2:19). Peter said that the Christian community, the church, was God's "holy nation" (1 Peter 2:9). The church has obviously become the spiritual equivalent in the New Testament of Israel in the Old Testament.

- When Jesus' disciples asked him about restoring the Kingdom to Israel, Jesus did not say, "The Kingdom is coming in the far future." Instead he told them that they would receive power to be his witnesses to the whole world (Acts 1:7 – 8). Jesus had warned Israel that if they did not receive him and his message, the Kingdom of God would be taken away from them and "given to a people who will produce its fruit" (Matthew 21:43). The New Testament does not predict a future restoration of Israel as a nation but teaches that Israelites can be saved in the same way non-Israelites are saved — by faith in Jesus Christ (Romans 11:23).

DiGGinG DeEPeR

If you want more detail on the premillennial position, read

✗ Campbell, Donald K., and Jeffrey Townsend. *The Coming Millennial Kingdom.* Grand Rapids: Kregel, 1997.

A classic commentary on Revelation from a premillennial viewpoint is

✗ Walvoord, John. *The Revelation of Jesus Christ.* Chicago: Moody Press, 1980.

Two books that explore all the major perspectives are

✗ Bock, Darrell L., ed. *Three Views on the Millennium and Beyond.* Grand Rapids: Zondervan, 1999.

✗ Clouse, Robert, ed. *The Meaning of the Millennium: Four Views.* Downers Grove, Ill.: InterVarsity Press, 1977.

HELP○FILE

ARE YOU CONVINCED — OR CONFUSED??

While all Christians agree that Jesus is the King and that he will return to earth in glory some day, the three views of God's Kingdom present three different pictures of what the future holds. The big question is — which view is right? Which of the three most accurately summarizes what the Bible teaches?

The view I accept is the premillennial view. Four facts convince me that it fits best with what the Bible says:

I'm agreeing with the witness of the early church. Almost every Christian teacher for the first three hundred years of the Christian church believed in a future Kingdom of God on earth. The men and women closest in time to the personal representatives of Jesus, his chosen apostles, were convinced that Jesus would reign over the earth after his return from heaven.

I'm interpreting the Bible in a consistently literal sense. The amillennial and postmillennial views consistently spiritualize the Old Testament prophecies and apply them to the church, the body they call the *spiritual Israel*. But all the Old Testament prophecies about Jesus' first coming were fulfilled literally. It only makes sense that the prophecies surrounding Jesus' second coming will also be fulfilled literally.

I'm acknowledging that God will keep all of his promises. Premillennialism is the only view that allows for the fulfillment of the promises God made to Abraham and David. God unconditionally promised Abraham that the whole world would be blessed through him and that his descendants would possess a specific piece of land forever. God unconditionally promised David that one of his descendants would rule over Israel forever. Since neither of these promises has been completely fulfilled in history, God will fulfill these promises in the future.

I'm reading Revelation 20:1-6 in its clearest sense. The premillennial position makes the most natural reading of John's words. Jesus' second coming is clearly before *(pre-)* the millennium in Revelation 20. Therefore, the premillennial framework for understanding the future seems to me most consistent with the Bible.

This doesn't mean, however, that I use my position to blast other Christians. Many godly, committed Christians hold other views, and I respect those who passionately believe and teach those views. They will not give an account to me for their faithfulness to Jesus; they will give an account to Jesus — and on that day we will *all* receive praise and reward from him.

Walking the Walk

The Bible was not given just to fill our minds and equip us for debates with other Christians. The Bible was given to change our lives! So how does our view of Christ's Kingdom affect our lives right now? Let me offer a few suggestions:

If You Hold to an Amillennial View of the Kingdom

Live right now as a loyal subject of the King. If Jesus reigns today as King, people around you should be able to see where your allegiance lies. If Jesus reigns over your church, your Christian community should be a

model of sacrificial love and humble ministry to a world in need.

Stay alert for Jesus' coming. Here are the words of King Jesus:

> No one knows about that day or hour, not even the angels in heaven, nor the Son, but only the Father. Be on guard! Be alert! You do not know when that time will come. It's like a man going away: He leaves his house and puts his servants in charge, each with his assigned task, and tells the one at the door to keep watch.
>
> Therefore keep watch because you do not know when the owner of the house will come back — whether in the evening, or at midnight, or when the rooster crows, or at dawn. If he comes suddenly, do not let him find you sleeping. What I say to you, I say to everyone: "Watch!"
>
> Mark 13:32 – 37

If You Hold to a Postmillennial View of the Kingdom

Be courageous in your presentation of the gospel. Jesus promised that the gates of hell would not stand against the power of the church. We must not huddle in fear inside our church fortresses. Jesus calls us to meet a hostile world with absolute confidence in the overcoming power of God's truth.

Work to address the social and spiritual diseases of our culture. The attacks against Christian morality are coming from all sides. Christians need to speak confidently, persuasively, lovingly, and passionately to a culture in desperate need of direction.

Points 2 Remember

- ☑ Jesus rules as God's King over all creation.

- ☑ Christians hold three views of the Kingdom. Disagreements center on two questions: *What* is the Kingdom like, and *when* does the Kingdom come?

- ☑ Your view of the Kingdom will have very practical effects on how you live each day.

If You Hold to a Premillennial View of the Kingdom

Live as though Jesus could return at any moment. When I was a teenager, my parents would say, just before I left for a date or to spend some time with my friends, "Go where you won't be ashamed for Jesus to find you." I thought it was corny then, but now it seems like very wise counsel.

Don't bring shame or disgrace on the cause of Christ by setting dates for the rapture or by sensationalizing every world event as a fulfillment of prophecy. Keep your hearts and minds focused on the big picture and on the clear promises of the Word.

Purify your life. The apostle John put it this way:

> We know that when [Jesus] appears, we shall be like him, for we shall see him as he is. Everyone who has this hope in him purifies himself, just as [Jesus] is pure.
>
> 1 John 3:2 – 3

Hebrews 12:28 – 29

Therefore, since we are receiving a kingdom that cannot be shaken, let us be thankful, and so worship God acceptably with reverence and awe, for our "God is a consuming fire."

MILLENNIAL VIEWS: HOW THEY STACK UP			
View	*When* **Jesus Will Reign**	*How* **Jesus Will Reign**	*Where* **Jesus Will Reign**
Amillennial	In the present age — *between* Jesus' first coming and second coming	Spiritual reign over the church and in the hearts of believers	In heaven
Postmillennial	In the future but *before* his return to earth	Spiritual and political reign through Christians on earth	In heaven
Premillennial	In the future but *after* his return to earth	Literal, personal reign over the Kingdom for a thousand years	On earth from his throne in Jerusalem

CHAPTER 8

Your Personal Future:
Death and What Comes After

Your Personal Future:
Death and What Comes After

— **Heads Up** ————————————————————

▸ Put "death" in your Day-Timer! It comes to all of us
▸ Is reincarnation an option? Have we all lived former lives?
▸ Physician-assisted suicide — medicine or murder?

The Bible's picture of the future isn't just about wars and evil empires. There's also a very personal part. *You* have a future too — and that future extends far beyond your life here on earth.

The doorway to that future is an experience most of us don't like to think about — we call it *death*. If you want to be left alone at a party, start asking people what they think death will be like. Your friends will find plenty of reasons to avoid you.

Everyone knows that death is inevitable. We just aren't very comfortable talking about it. This doesn't mean, however, that we aren't interested in death. Most of us really do want to know what death brings and what lies beyond.

Information about death is not hard to find. Just visit your local bookstore. The author of some best-selling book will claim to give you the answers. Someone who has "died" and come back to life will be happy to tell you all about the dark tunnel and the bright light. Television talk shows regularly feature people who have had a near-death or after-death experience. Nor will you have any trouble locating Internet sites about "life after death."

Information about death is not the problem. What is hard to find is *reliable* information about death and about what comes next. I don't know about you, but when I stand at the casket of someone I love or when I face death myself, I want more than just someone's *opinion* about death. I want some facts. Another person's experience won't bring me much comfort either. My experience may or may not be like someone else's. I want some assurance of what I will face. When I die, am I done for? Is that the end? If I live on, where will I be?

Fortunately, there is one person who has passed through death and come back to tell us about it — and his word can be trusted! Jesus walked into the jaws of death, stripped it of its power, and conquered it forever through his resurrection. In addition, Jesus beamed a clear, bright light into the darkness beyond death, and he lets us see what's waiting for us there.

Why We Die

The word *death* is used in the Bible to describe three different conditions or experiences. The central idea in each case is separation. Death always involved separation.

The first condition we encounter in the Bible is *spiritual death* — the separation of a person from a relationship with God. Spiritual death is the present condition of every person who has not believed in Jesus as Savior and Lord. That's why we need to be born again by faith in Jesus Christ. Spiritually dead people need new life.

The word *death* is also used in the Bible to describe *physical death* — the separation of the human spirit from the human body. At death, the nonphysical part of us (the spirit or the soul) leaves the physical body.

The third condition called "death" in the Bible is the *second death* — the final and permanent separation of a person from God.

The Bible also gives us some insight into why we die. Every death has its own story. If you look beyond the obituary, you will discover at least three causes for every human death.

"It's not that I'm afraid to die. I just don't want to be there when it happens."

Woody Allen, actor, director, comedian

Quotation Marks

We're most familiar with the "immediate cause of death." This can be any number of things — a heart attack, stroke, cancer, drowning, a car accident. The immediate cause of death is what we hear about on the news when a death is reported.

TAKING IT TO EXTREMES

In 1959 Jim Jones had a vision that Indianapolis, Indiana, would be destroyed in a great catastrophe. Eventually Jones claimed to be God in human form, and he led his followers to a jungle compound in Guyana, South America. On November 18, 1978, Jones ordered a mass suicide that claimed the lives of more than nine hundred men, women, and children.

Victor Howell, the leader of an offshoot of the Seventh-Day Adventists that called itself the Branch Davidians, changed his name to David Koresh. The name was a combination of the name of Israel's great king (David) and the name of a Persian commander (Cyrus — *koresh* in Hebrew). David Koresh claimed to be the Lamb of Revelation 5, the second incarnation of Jesus Christ. On February 28, 1993, the Bureau of Alcohol, Firearms, and Tobacco stormed the group's compound in Waco, Texas. After a fifty-one-day standoff, the FBI put the compound under siege. Fire broke out and quickly engulfed the buildings. About one hundred Branch Davidians died, including seventeen children.

In 1534 Jan Bockelson, also called John of Leyden, declared that he was the Messiah and that the German city of Münster was the new Jerusalem. Like so many cult movements before and since, this one ended in disaster. Catholic armies besieged the city, and in September 1534 the army broke through and massacred Bockelson's followers. Bockelson and two of his lieutenants were hung in iron cages — food for the birds. The cages are still around! Thousands of tourists flock to see them every year.

But more is going on than just a heart attack. A second factor behind physical death is the moral cause of the death. When our parents Adam and Eve disobeyed God's command in the Garden of Eden, one of the consequences was death. (You can read the story in Genesis 3.) Human sin put the whole creation under a shroud. Sickness, pain, suffering, and despair are now part of the human condition (Romans 5:12; James 1:15). If you've ever wondered why children suffer abuse or why at times the best people experience the harshest deaths — these cruel situations all occur as the consequence of living in a sin-cursed, sin-filled world.

Beyond the immediate and the moral causes of death stands the ultimate cause. The one who bears final responsibility for death is God: "The LORD brings death and makes alive; he brings down to the grave and raises up" (1 Samuel 2:6; see also Job 34:14 – 15; Acts 17:28).

Bright Light on a Dark Path

The Bible tells us what death is like by painting some pictures — not with watercolors but with words. Each image is designed to bring us comfort and peace as we think about death. If you are terrified by the thought of death, begin to replace those fearful images with God's pictures of what death will bring.

The Bible most often pictures death as *sleep* (2 Chronicles 9:31; Psalm 13:3; Daniel 12:2; John 11:11 – 13; 1 Corinthians 11:30; 15:51). Death, like sleep, is temporary and ends in a great awakening. I think the Bible uses the image of sleep so often because both sleep and death are universal experiences. From birth to old age, human beings need sleep. When I'm tired, I look forward to lying down and letting sleep sweep over me. We don't fear sleep; we welcome it, and we eagerly anticipate a new day.

Jesus described his death as an *exodus*, a joyful liberation (Luke 9:31). Death would like to keep us in bondage and fear, but Jesus died to set us free (Romans 5:14, 21; Hebrews 2:14 – 15). Our death is not a descent into darkness but a joy-filled release from the pain and disappointment of this life.

Death is also like *taking down a tent*. Our bodies are our temporary dwelling places — "the earthly tent we live in" (2 Corinthians 5:1). In these bodies we are subject to disease and distress and despair. But Christians are confident that when this earthly tent is folded up in death, "we have a building from God, an eternal house in heaven" (2 Corinthians 5:1). Death is the first step in the process that will bring us to a permanent, changed-forever body that will never age or require a wheelchair.

I think I'm most comforted by the Bible's portrayal of death as *coming home*. To the minds of most of us, home represents a place of acceptance and rest and security. When our spirit separates from our body in death, we find ourselves "at home with the Lord" (2 Corinthians 5:8). For the Christian, home is a place we've never been.

The apostle Paul thought of death as a *departure* (Philippians 1:22 – 24; 2 Timothy 4:6). We pull up the anchor, untie the ropes holding us to

HELP FILE

NEAR-DEATH EXPERIENCES: ARE THEY FOR REAL?

The Bible isn't the only book to talk about death. Look over the best-sellers at your local Barnes and Noble bookstores, and you'll likely find someone's near-death or after-death story.

I'm pretty skeptical of near-death claims. I don't question the person's honesty or even the claim that he or she had some dramatic experience. My question is whether this experience accurately reflected what death is really like. Did the person actually die? Medically we have no way of knowing when the spirit leaves the body, so we can't say when death occurs. Most of the characteristic features of near-death experiences — the sense of leaving your body, movement through a dark tunnel toward a bright light, a sense of warmth and peace, a review of life's events — have been linked to a lack of oxygen or even to the loss of certain brain functions brought on by the stress or trauma of a physical crisis.

Another difficulty I have with near-death experiences is the result of a statement in the Bible in Hebrews 9:27. It says there that a person dies only *once*. I realize that there have been some notable exceptions to this rule. Jesus' friend Lazarus had been dead for four days when Jesus raised him from the dead (John 11:38 – 44). Lazarus later died physically a second time. But if you add up all the people who were raised to life in the Bible and who had to die a second time, only fifteen or twenty people in all of history have had that experience. And none of them ever said a word about what happened while they were dead! No books, no appearances on Oprah. It seems hard to believe that, suddenly in the last few years, God is bringing hundreds of people through death and then back to life again.

I'm convinced that a lot of what we hear about near-death experiences is Satan's attempt to deceive people about what really lies beyond death's door. There's nothing like the prospect of death and of personal accountability to God to make us seriously consider the claims of Jesus Christ and our own destiny. If people believe, however, based on a few near-death encounters, that death will lead them to a place of love and acceptance regardless of their relationship to Jesus, they will no longer be motivated to evaluate their lives. The attraction of God's saving grace invariably fades if a person is deceived into thinking he or she does not need saving.

this life, and sail away. It's not a departure to an unknown destination. We depart to be with Christ.

The Bible doesn't promise this kind of death to everyone. These pictures and promises are for those who have believed in Jesus Christ as Savior. If you have never personally trusted Jesus, you *should* be terrified of death. You will face death all alone, and you will find yourself in an eternity separated from God. The good news is that you don't have to live in fear of death. God offers you eternal life right now if you in faith receive Jesus Christ as your Savior and Lord. This life doesn't start after you die; you experience a whole new kind of life the moment you believe.

What Are My Other Options?

Not everyone agrees on what happens after we die. Just ask the people you work with what they think will happen after death. If you ask ten friends, you'll end up with eleven opinions.

People who reject the Bible's position that after death we continue to live a conscious existence in another place usually embrace one of the following alternatives:

Reincarnation

I listened to a lecture a few years ago given by a woman who claimed she had lived hundreds of lives. She could even remember a few of them. She had been a male commander in the army of Joshua, the biblical general. She had also been a medieval Waldensian girl who had been dragged by the neck and then burned at the stake for her faith. Quite a claim!

The belief that human beings are reborn to earthly existence after death is not new. The idea of reincarnation first appeared in early Hindu writings about 1000 B.C. More than one-fourth of all Americans accept some form of reincarnation as possible.

Biblical Christianity has always rejected reincarnation — with very good reason. Human beings are not progressing upward to God through a long cycle of rebirths. The Bible says that we are disoriented and lost, dead in our sins, and separated from God. What redeems us from this dreadful situation are the wonderful grace and forgiveness of God.

When Jesus was crucified, a thief on the cross next to him admitted his own sin and asked Jesus to remember him with favor in the future Kingdom of God. Jesus did not promise the man a higher incarnation in his next life. Jesus said instead, "Today you will be with me in paradise" (Luke 23:43).

I think reincarnation is becoming more widely accepted because it's convenient to believe. It is easier to think that you will return to another human life than that you will give an account to God for the life you are living right now. Reincarnation also appeals to human pride by teaching that a person's final destiny rests on human effort, not on the grace or judgment of God.

The woman who believed that she had lived hundreds of lives may have been sincere in her belief, but she was sincerely wrong! The testimony of the Bible shows that reincarnation is not the truth about what happens after death.

Soul Sleep

Some religious groups teach that at death the soul sleeps, just like the body sleeps. Their argument is that a human being is a unit — body and soul (or spirit) functioning *together* to make a person. Therefore, when the body ceases to function, so does the soul. In this view, the body and the soul sleep until the resurrection, when the full person (body and soul) is awakened to face either the glory of heaven or the condemnation of hell. Since the soul has no consciousness in death, it *seems* as though we are immediately in Christ's presence when we die, but in reality we aren't.

The New Testament, however, makes it clear that our spirits will exist in consciousness, apart from our bodies. In the apostle John's vision

Hebrews 9:27

Everyone has to die once, then face the consequences.

Eugene Peterson, THE MESSAGE

SUICIDES IN THE BIBLE

- Abimelech, the son of Gideon, ordered his armor-bearer to kill him after he had been fatally wounded by a millstone that was dropped on his head (Judges 9:54).
- Samson, a later judge of Israel, brought down a building, killing himself and hundreds of Philistines (Judges 16:26 – 30).
- Israel's first king, Saul, fell on his own sword after being mortally wounded in battle (1 Samuel 31:4).
- Saul's armor-bearer refused Saul's request to kill the king but killed himself, just as Saul had done (1 Samuel 31:5). The armor-bearer career track was a tough one, indeed!
- Ahithophel, a traitor to King David, hanged himself when David's rebellious son, Absalom, rejected his advice (2 Samuel 17:23).
- An evil king of Israel, Zimri, set the palace on fire and died after reigning for only seven days (1 Kings 16:18).
- Judas Iscariot hanged himself after betraying Jesus (Matthew 27:5).

of heaven, he saw under the altar "the *souls* of those who had been slain" (emphasis added). These souls cried out to God, understood God's reply, and were consciously aware of events, both in heaven and on earth (Revelation 6:9 – 11). In Philippians 1:23 – 24, Paul makes a clear distinction between being "in the body" here on earth and being "with Christ" after death. The concept of soul sleep seems to me to be an inadequate explanation of our existence after death.

Annihilation

Many people in our world think that when we die we simply cease to exist. We've already seen that the Bible clearly contradicts that view. As much as human beings may want to deny it, death is not the end of a person's existence.

The Christian view of suicide contrasts dramatically with the view — one being adopted by a larger and larger segment of our society — that suicide is a heroic act. When a rock singer or film star decides to "check out" or "trip out" fatally, he or she is revered as someone who has made the greatest sacrifice or who has registered the boldest protest against a meaningless existence. More and more young people find suicide to be a compelling end to a life they feel is empty or aimless.

What If the Suffering Is Unbearable?

Most of us don't fear death as much as we fear what may be involved in the process of dying. We've seen family members or friends die long, painful deaths from disease or disability, and our thought is, *Please, God, take me quickly when it's time for me to die.*

Several elements in our culture have stepped forward with a "solution" to the suffering of those who are terminally ill or who have crippling, painful diseases. They advocate "physician-assisted suicide" — medical professionals granted permission to legally administer lethal doses of medication to patients who have chosen to end their own lives. Physician-assisted suicide is portrayed as humane ("it ends human suffering") and as the supreme exercise of individual liberty ("he or she has a right to die").

Quotation Marks

The most powerful words about suicide I've ever read were written by Anne-Grace Scheinin, who wrestled with thoughts of suicide for several years and twice had seriously attempted it. Then her own mother killed herself, and she experienced the pain firsthand. As a survivor, Scheinin writes haunting words — words to remember if (or when) the tempter whispers the fatal suggestion in your ears:

"I'm alive because of my mother's death. She taught me that, in spite of my illness, I had to live. Suicide just isn't worth it.

"I saw the torment my mother's death caused others: my father, my brother, her neighbors and friends. When I saw their overwhelming grief, I knew I could never do the same thing she had done — force other people to take on the burden of pain I'd leave behind if I died by my own hand.

"Suicide is not a normal death. It is tragic beyond the most shattering experiences, and the ultimate form of abandonment.

"[My mother] taught me the most valuable lesson of my life: No matter how bad the pain is, it's never so bad that suicide is the only answer. It's never so bad that the only escape is a false one. Suicide doesn't end pain. It only lays it on the broken shoulders of the survivors."

Anne-Grace Scheinin, "The Burden of Suicide,"
Newsweek, 7 February 1983, 13

From a biblical viewpoint, physician-assisted suicide is indefensible because it is based on unbiblical foundations.

First, advocates claim that death ends human suffering. Death certainly does end physical suffering for those who are in Christ, but death will usher some people into a place of torment. Many of those who support physician-assisted suicide spout off angrily against the "religious" arguments raised about the practice. They want society to take a purely secular approach to the issue and leave religious or biblical issues out of the debate.

The second foundation on which support for physician-assisted suicide rests is the claim that death and the circumstances of death are matters that we as human beings have the right and authority to choose for ourselves. But the Bible consistently says that the opposite is true. Death and life are the sole prerogatives of God. Listen to an ancient wise man named Job: "Man's days are determined;

Points 2 Remember

☑ Jesus has conquered death forever. We don't have to fear what lies beyond.

☑ For a Christian, death is joyful liberation into the presence of Jesus Christ.

☑ Suicide is never the right answer to pain and suffering. It only inflicts more pain on those who are left behind.

DEATH BY CHOICE

Seven suicides are recorded in the Bible, and they are all portrayed as tragic, desperate events. The most notorious biblical suicide was the one committed by Judas Iscariot after he had betrayed Jesus. Suicide is never explicitly condemned in Scripture as a crime or a sin, but throughout the history of the church, suicide has never been regarded as an act that pleases God. The most influential biblical statement has been the sixth commandment: "You shall not murder" (Exodus 20:13; Matthew 19:18; Romans 13:9). Since suicide is self-murder, it is an act that clearly violates God's command.

you have decreed the number of his months and have set limits he cannot exceed" (Job 14:5; see also Psalm 139:16).

But does God really want us to experience prolonged suffering if we are going to die anyway? The third foundation used to support physician-assisted suicide is the claim that it is an act of compassion to bring an end to prolonged and painful suffering. How can we ignore the pleadings of those who want to die?

Several individuals in the Bible were so sick or depressed that it appeared to them (and to others) that they would die — but they didn't die. In fact, great blessing came into their lives after they recovered! Check out the full story of Job (the book of Job) and the Bible's account of Elijah's depression (1 Kings 19).

I've stood beside too many bedsides and watched too many people suffer through long months — even years — of pain to be heartless or unsympathetic about this issue. I am simply forced by my understanding of God's truth to conclude that the deliberate termination of human life is wrong. Human beings are made in the image of God, and we have no right to arbitrarily take life for the sake of convenience or choice. Christians will have to make expensive, difficult, sacrificial choices to protect life as each generation ages, but the alternative is to see our society plunge into a total disregard for all human life that is considered unnecessary or too burdensome.

DiGGinG DeEpeR

- ✗ Lewis, C. S. *A Grief Observed*. San Francisco: HarperSanFrancisco, 1994.
  A classic remembrance of the pain the death of a loved one brings.

- ✗ Kreeft, Peter. *Between Heaven and Hell*. Downers Grove, Ill.: InterVarsity Press, 1982.
  A dramatic imaginary conversation about death, with John F. Kennedy, C. S. Lewis, and Aldous Huxley (these three men died within a few hours of each other).

- ✗ Sproul, R. C. *Surprised by Suffering*. Wheaton, Ill.: Tyndale House, 1989.
  An in-depth study of death and what follows.

The Other Side of Death's Door

Death is not the end; it is simply the doorway to a whole new realm of existence. Jesus and the Bible are consistent in saying that there are only two options after we die: We either go into the presence of Jesus, or we go to a place of separation from Jesus. That's it — two roads, two ends, two destinies. And once we are in one of these two places, there's no possibility of change. The Bible never holds out the slightest hope of a second chance to believe in Jesus after death. The decisions that affect our eternal destinies are made in this life, not after we die.

So put "death" in your Day-Timer! It will come someday. Every day you are building the legacy you will leave behind. Your destiny after death depends on just one thing — your faith relationship with Jesus Christ. Popular truth? No. Truth? Yes!

CHAPTER 9

Judgment Day: Everyone's Future Accountability to God

Judgment Day: Everyone's Future Accountability to God

— Heads Up —

- ▸ We all face the Judge
- ▸ Rewards in heaven
- ▸ Hell: A place you *don't* want to visit

Some people do good things and never get recognized. Teachers, parents, police officers, medical personnel, and everyday Good Samaritans do heroic deeds and make enormous sacrifices, but they never have their names in lights or even in the newspaper headlines.

Other people do bad things — horrific things — and never pay the price. Oppressive dictators retire in luxury; war criminals and terrorists are treated like heroes; child molesters evade arrest and live long lives. It just isn't fair! Where's the justice?

The Bible makes it clear that not every account is settled in this life on this earth. Every person faces a future evaluation — and no one will escape. The judge in charge will know every fact fully and honestly. The hidden motives and intentions behind every act and every word will be obvious to him. No legal technicality will get a person off the hook. The law will be absolutely just and without appeal. Some people face this future evaluation with joy; many face it with dread. What makes the difference is *your relationship with the judge*.

Here Come da Judge!

God the Father has given the responsibility of judging human beings to one person — to God the Son, namely, Jesus Christ. But don't just take my word for it. Here's what Jesus said:

> Moreover, the Father judges no one, but has entrusted all judgment to the Son....
>
> And [the Father] has given [the Son] authority to judge because he is the Son of Man....
>
> I judge only as I hear, and my judgment is just. (John 5:22, 27, 30)

God the Father entrusted the judgment of human beings to Jesus in order to be fair. If God the Father was the judge, human beings could say, "You don't know what it's like to live where we live. You don't know how hard it is to resist sin's tempting power." No one can say that to Jesus.

Jesus became fully human when he came to this earth. He wasn't God pretending to be human. He was the real thing. Furthermore, Jesus was tempted in every area of life in which we face temptation. (Check out Hebrews 2:17 – 18; 4:15.) If you struggle with sexual temptation, Jesus faced the same enticement. If you battle with desires for intoxicating drugs, Jesus faced those same urges to escape reality. Anger, theft, the desire for money, gossip, prejudice, revenge — whatever gnaws away at your life — Jesus had to stand against these, too.

The result is that Jesus understands us from the inside. He never gave in to the temptation, but he felt its power. He can be a sympathetic, understanding judge because *he has been here with us.*

The Father also entrusted Jesus with the whole judgment scene because *Jesus is God.* He won't be fogged by someone's smooth words. He won't miss crucial pieces of evidence. Jesus will know everything about us — every thought, every motive, every detail. He will be fair, but also honest and just.

Jesus' judgment is also certain. It's a sure thing. No one will escape: "For [God] has set a day when he will judge the world with justice by the man he has appointed" (Acts 17:31).

Doomsday

Christians all agree that every person will give an account of his or her life to God and will be rewarded or condemned. Christians disagree on *when* God's judgment will take place.

The most widely held view is that one final judgment will cover everyone. All men and women of all time who have believed God's truth will be rewarded and ushered into the glories of heaven; all men and women of all time who have rejected God's truth will be condemned and separated from God in hell.

Some Scripture passages seem to point to one big judgment day:

> A time is coming when all who are in their graves will hear his voice and come out — those who have done good will rise to live, and those who have done evil will rise to be condemned. (John 5:28 – 29)

> Multitudes who sleep in the dust of the earth will awake: some to everlasting life, others to shame and everlasting contempt. (Daniel 12:2)

In those instances where the Bible seems to point out differences in the judgments, those who hold to a onetime, all-inclusive judgment say that the Bible is just highlighting different aspects of the same final judgment. Other Christians believe that the different aspects of God's judgment actually point to several different judgments at different times in God's program. We will *all* give an account to God — just not all at the same time.

I think a fairly strong case can be made for several judgments in God's future program — in fact, at least six individual times of judgment.

The Judgment of the Cross

One of God's major judgments is already finished. When Jesus died on the cross, Satan's doom and the condemnation of all who follow Satan in his rebellion against God were sealed. Jesus said, "Now is the time for judgment on this world; now the prince of this world will be driven out" (John 12:31). Satan used every deceptive tactic he could think of to get Jesus to avoid the cross, but nothing turned Jesus away from doing the Father's will. The death of Jesus as the full sacrifice for human sin resulted in sealing Satan's destiny in the lake of fire (Revelation 20:10). Because of the cross, "the prince of this world now stands condemned" (John 16:11).

Remember this when Satan comes to you with one of his deceptive suggestions designed to turn you from the path of obedience and love

BELIEVERS PAST, BELIEVERS FUTURE

New Testament Church-Age believers aren't the only ones who will face an evaluation before Jesus. Those true believers who died before Jesus' death and resurrection will face one, too. Their spirits are already in heaven, but their bodies will not be resurrected until Jesus returns to earth at the end of the Tribulation. Old Testament believers were not looking for the rapture like we, as New Testament believers, are. Old Testament believers looked for the coming of the Messiah's glorious Kingdom on earth. Abraham and Job and Ruth will be resurrected and ushered directly into this Kingdom (Daniel 12:1 – 2). We assume that they will face an evaluation in which their faithfulness to God will be rewarded.

The same can be said about those who believe in Jesus during the Tribulation. Many of them will be killed — martyred — for their loyalty to Jesus Christ. Tribulation believers will be resurrected and rewarded at the end of the Tribulation and will reign with Jesus during the thousand-year Kingdom (Revelation 20:4 – 6).

for God. He's already a defeated enemy! The Holy Spirit living in you is far greater than Satan and all his forces (1 John 4:4).

The Judgment Seat of Christ

The first judgment in the future will involve Christians — all the followers of Jesus from the time of Jesus' death and resurrection until Christians are removed from the earth in the rapture. Every Christian, one by one, will stand before the Savior who died for us.

> For we must all appear before the judgment seat of Christ, that each one may receive what is due him for the things done while in the body, whether good or bad. (2 Corinthians 5:10)

> We will all stand before God's judgment seat.... Each of us will give an account of himself to God. (Romans 14:10, 12)

Keep several facts in mind as you read these verses. First, Jesus' evaluation of our lives is *not* to determine whether we enter heaven or not. The issue of our eternal destiny was settled when we believed in Jesus and received eternal life by his grace alone. Second, we will not face condemnation or punishment for our sins when we stand before Jesus. God has promised that no condemnation will ever fall on those who are in Christ Jesus by faith (John 5:21; Romans 8:1). The final fact to remember is that this evaluation will focus on what we did in life with the gifts, resources, and opportunities God gave us. The outcome of this evaluation will be either reward or loss of reward — or, to use a New Testament image, the "building" we have constructed in this life will either burn up or bring us honor from Jesus himself:

> By the grace God has given me, I laid a foundation as an expert builder, and someone else is building on it. But each one should be careful how he builds. For no one can lay any foundation other than the one already laid, which is Jesus Christ. If any man builds on this foundation using gold, silver, costly stones, wood, hay or straw, his work will be shown for what it is, because the Day will bring it to light. It will be revealed with fire, and the fire will test the quality of each man's work. If what he has built survives, he will receive his reward. If it is burned up, he will suffer loss; he himself will be saved, but only as one escaping through the flames. (1 Corinthians 3:10 – 15)

Whether you know it or not, whether you like it or not, you *are* building on God's construction project. The foundation of the building was set when Jesus died on the cross, the blueprint has been approved by God himself, and each one of us is building.

What Paul emphasizes in this passage is that we have a choice of building materials. We can use eternal things to build with, or we can use worthless things. Gold, silver, and costly stones refer to Christ-honoring motives, personal integrity, and joyful obedience to God. Wood, hay, and straw are perishable things — sinful pursuits, selfish motives, pride-filled actions, underhanded manipulation. If you are

Quotation Marks

"Imagine staring into the face of Christ. Just the two of you, one-on-one! Your entire life is present before you. In a flash you see what he sees. No hiding. No opportunity to put a better spin on what you did. No attorney to represent you. The look in his eyes says it all. Like it or not, that is precisely where you and I shall be someday."

Erwin Lutzer, in *Your Eternal Reward* (Chicago: Moody Press, 1998), 23

1 John 2:28

And now, dear children, continue in [Jesus], so that when he appears we may be confident and unashamed before him at his coming.

seeking to serve God with commitment and in obedience, you are building with the right stuff. If you are coasting along with no desire for spiritual growth or no demonstration of sacrificial ministry to others, you are building on God's house with the wrong stuff.

My part of the building will be examined by Jesus himself and tested by the fire of his heart-searching gaze. This fire will expose and destroy all the things I have done out of selfish ambition and with wrong motives. Some of these things may look, to all outward appearances, like very noble and even sacrificial deeds, but Jesus will reveal the secret intentions behind them. On the other hand, the fire will expose other actions as true acts of humility and worth, even though they appear at first to be pretty insignificant. You and I will be rewarded on the basis of what remains. The gold, silver, and costly stones of obedience and faithfulness will be transformed into crowns of reward.

CROWNS

The word used in the Bible for a Christian's rewards is not the word for a king's crown but the word for the wreath given to the winner in an athletic contest. The rewards will be visible evidence of faithfulness to the Lord. But we won't wear these crowns for long! We will lay them before the Lord in recognition of his grace and his love for us (Revelation 4:10).

Here are the different crowns mentioned in the Bible:

Crown of life for enduring through trial (James 1:12; Revelation 2:10)

Crown of righteousness for those who eagerly look for Jesus' return and live obedient lives in light of his coming (2 Timothy 4:8)

Crown of glory for servant leaders (1 Peter 5:4)

The incorruptible crown for consistent self-discipline (1 Corinthians 9:24 – 27)

Crown of rejoicing for faithfully sharing the gospel and bringing people to faith in Jesus Christ (1 Thessalonians 2:19)

The whole picture of the judgment seat of Christ comes straight out of the athletic games of the New Testament world. After the races and games concluded, a dignitary — or even the emperor himself — took his seat on an elevated throne in the arena. One by one the winning athletes came up to the throne to receive a reward — usually a wreath of leaves, a victor's crown.

Some Christians are bothered by the idea of rewards or crowns for faithful obedience to Jesus Christ. The apostle Paul certainly wasn't ashamed to strive for rewards. He served Christ first and foremost out of love for Christ, but he also had a burning passion to receive Christ's approval on his life.

I'm not sure *when* each believer will stand before Jesus Christ. Some Christians think we will all be evaluated just after the rapture. It's certainly possible that Christians who die before the rapture face the evaluation immediately after death. What's important to remember is that the judgment seat of Christ is not an encounter we should fear. We will stand before the person who loves us with a boundless love, and his perfect love will drive out our fear (1 John 4:18). But the fact that we will give an account of our lives to Christ should make us realize how serious the Lord is about how we live our lives as his children.

The Bible makes one other point I can't skip over. Some of us will receive rewards at our future evaluation, and some of us will experience the loss of our rewards (1 Corinthians 3:14 – 15). Jesus will show us what *could* have been our reward if we had only served him more

Bible NetWorking
Essential Reading on the Judgment Seat of Christ

1 Corinthians 3:1 – 15	Matthew 20:1 – 16	1 Corinthians 9:24 – 27
2 Timothy 4:7 – 8	Matthew 25:14 – 30	Philippians 3:14
James 5:8 – 9	Romans 14:10, 12	
1 John 2:28	2 Corinthians 5:10	

faithfully, but all we will have to offer him will be ashes, the burned-up remains of laziness or the fruits of selfish motives. We will be saved — but unrewarded. What a tragedy to stand with empty hands as we look at his nail-pierced hands!

The Judgment of the Antichrist and His Armies

God's judgment will pummel a rebellious world for the entire seven years of the Tribulation. But at the end of the Tribulation, when Jesus returns from heaven in glory, several specific judgments will fall.

The Antichrist, an evil ruler set on world conquest, will gather a massive army in the nation of Israel for one final assault on the followers of Jesus and on the Jewish people living in Jerusalem. (See chapters 4 and 6 for more details on how the events of the Tribulation fit together.) For a while, it seems certain that the Antichrist will crush all those opposed to him. But then the heavens open, and Jesus returns to earth in victory.

"ONE WILL BE TAKEN AND THE OTHER LEFT"

Two men will be in the field; one will be taken and the other left. Two women will be grinding with a hand mill; one will be taken and the other left.

Matthew 24:40 – 41

These verses have usually been quoted as a description of the rapture, the time when Jesus returns in the air for his people and takes them to heaven. But Jesus was *not* talking here about the rapture! Jesus was talking about his return to earth at the end of the Tribulation. At that time another "rapture" takes place — but in reverse. Instead of God's people being removed, the wicked and unbelieving will be removed. Jesus will send his angels out, and they will remove evil people from the earth. The one "left behind" on that occasion will enter Jesus' Kingdom on earth.

Jesus said that the world would be like a field where wheat and weeds grow up together. At the end of the age, the "weeds" are pulled up and destroyed: "The Son of Man will send out his angels, and they will weed out of his kingdom everything that causes sin and all who do evil" (Matthew 13:41). The believers who are left on earth "will shine like the sun in the kingdom of their Father" (Matthew 13:43).

For the entire parable Jesus told to convey these events, read Matthew 13:24 – 30, 36 – 43. The parable of the fishing net makes the same point — Matthew 13:47 – 50.

REGATHERED ISRAEL

One of the promises repeated most often in the Old Testament is God's promise to gather the family of Israel back to the land of Palestine as a permanent home. (Click on Isaiah 11:11 – 12; 43:5 – 6; Jeremiah 30:10; 31:27 – 28; 33:14 – 16; Ezekiel 36:24 – 38).

The regathering of Israel began in 1948 with the creation of the modern state of Israel. But the Jews are gathering in unbelief, and during the future Tribulation Israel will be scattered again. When Jesus returns, how-ever, all Israel will be gathered back to the land God promised to Abraham.

The Lord doesn't make it easy for the people who have rejected him. He will not allow them to enter the joy of the earthly Kingdom until he has entered into judgment with them (Jeremiah 30:11; 31:1 – 14; Zechariah 13:8 – 9). Those who pass under the "rod" of Christ's judgment successfully will inherit the promised Kingdom (Ezekiel 20:37; 34:20 – 31).

The Antichrist (called "the beast" in Revelation) and his sidekick, the false prophet, are condemned to the lake of burning sulfur: "Then I saw the beast and the kings of the earth and their armies gathered together to make war against the rider on the horse [that is, Jesus returning from heaven] and his army. But the beast was captured, and with him the false prophet.... The two of them were thrown alive into the fiery lake of burning sulfur" (Revelation 19:19 – 20).

The armies of the Antichrist die at Jesus' spoken word of judgment: "The rest of them were killed with the sword that came out of the mouth of the rider on the horse, and all the birds gorged themselves on their flesh" (Revelation 19:21).

As powerful in appearance as the Antichrist will be on the earth during the Tribulation, he's no match for Jesus. Jesus will overthrow him "with the breath of his mouth" and destroy his evil empire simply "by the splendor of his coming" (2 Thessalonians 2:8). One puff of air from Jesus sends Satan's greatest instruments to hell.

The Judgment of the Survivors of the Tribulation

Millions of people will die during the Tribulation — but millions will survive! Some of them will be loyal followers of the Antichrist; a few will be faithful followers of Jesus who have managed to escape the

THE BOOK OF LIFE

The book of life is a record opened at the final judgment of all unbelieving people (Revelation 20:11 – 12). The book contains the names of those who have believed in Jesus as Savior and Lord. Those who have not believed do not have their names written in the book.

Every person who stands condemned before God will see with his or her own eyes that his or her name does not appear in God's book. Instead, these individuals will be judged according to other "books," which will demonstrate beyond any doubt that, in spite of repeated opportunities to believe in Jesus, they consistently rejected his grace. No one will raise an argument against God's convincing justice.

Antichrist's reign of terror. The Old Testament prophet Daniel implies that Jesus will take about two and a half months after his return to judge those still living on the earth and to sweep away all the remnants of the Antichrist's evil rule (Daniel 12:11 – 12).

Jewish people will be regathered from all over the world into the desert of Israel. They will then be judged individually by the Messiah, whom their ancestors had rejected and killed. Those Jews who believe in Jesus and receive him as their Sovereign Lord will enter the thousand-year Kingdom. Those who have received the mark of the beast and those who refuse to believe in Jesus as the Messiah will die (Ezekiel 20:33 – 44; Malachi 4:1 – 3; Revelation 14:9).

The non-Jewish people (Gentiles) who survive the Tribulation will be gathered in the Valley of Jehoshaphat (je-**hosh**-a-fat), east of the city of Jerusalem. Those who have believed in Jesus and have been faithful to him throughout the Tribulation will be ushered into Jesus' earthly Kingdom. Those who have received the Antichrist's mark or who refuse to believe will die (Joel 3:1 – 3; Matthew 25:31 – 46; Revelation 14:9).

The Judgment of Satan and Evil Angels

The beginning of the end for Satan comes in the middle of the Tribulation when Satan and his angels are cast out of heaven and confined to the earth (Revelation 12:7 – 9). At the beginning of the thousand-year Kingdom, Satan is confined to a place the Bible calls the Abyss, a spiritual prison. Satan's release at the end of the thousand years leads to one final rebellion on earth, which God quickly crushes (Revelation 20:1 – 3).

Finally the day will come when Satan and the angels who have followed him in defiance of God will be judged (2 Peter 2:4; Jude 6). As amazing as it sounds, Christians will have some role to play in this judgment on the angels (1 Corinthians 6:3: "Do you not know that we will judge angels?"; see also Romans 16:20). In the end, even Satan will bow his knee to Jesus and agree that Jesus is Lord over all (Philippians 2:9 – 11). Then Satan and his evil forces will be sent to the lake of fire forever (Revelation 20:10).

The Judgment of All Unbelievers

The final judgment of all time is the *great white throne judgment* — the awesome day when those who have rejected God's grace face condemnation and separation from God forever:

> Then I saw a great white throne and him who was seated on it. Earth and sky fled from his presence, and there was no place for them. And I saw the dead, great and small, standing before the throne, and books were opened. Another book was opened, which is the book of life. The dead were judged according to what they had done as recorded in the books. The sea gave up the dead that were in it, and death and Hades gave up the dead that were in them, and each person was judged according to what he had done. Then death and Hades were thrown into the lake of fire. The lake of fire is the second death. If anyone's name was not found written in the book of life, he was thrown into the lake of fire. (Revelation 20:11 – 15)

At this point in God's plan — at the very end of the thousand-year reign of Christ on earth — all the believers throughout all of history have already been raised from the dead and given glorified eternal bodies. The

Points 2 Remember

- ☑ Every person will someday stand before God in judgment.

- ☑ Jesus, God the Son, will judge everyone with perfect justice.

- ☑ Believers in Jesus will have their lives evaluated at the judgment seat of Christ to receive rewards or to lose rewards.

- ☑ Those outside of Jesus Christ will be condemned at the great white throne judgment. Their penalty will be eternal separation from the presence and the care of God.

only people whose bodies are still in the grave are those who have not believed the message of God's grace. Unbelieving men and women from creation until the time of the final rebellion will be raised to life and will stand before the Judge whose love and deliverance they had refused to accept. Those who chose to live without God in this life will find themselves separated from him forever.

The people who stand at the great white throne are not judged to see whether they will go to heaven or hell. They made that decision when they chose to live their own way rather than God's way. They are judged "according to what they had done" (Revelation 20:12). Unbelieving men and women will be judged to determine their degree of accountability and responsibility before God. Perhaps their punishment in eternity will vary, depending on how much of God's truth each individual understood and yet rejected. One thing is certain — all the works that are recorded in God's books will do nothing more than confirm their choice to reject all that God had offered them.

The resurrection to condemnation and God's final judgment will conclude with an act of ultimate separation. Every unbeliever's knee will bow to Jesus Christ, and every individual will confess that Jesus is Lord, and then every person who has rejected God's grace will be ushered into the lake of fire. No description of that place is easy to read:

> They will be punished with everlasting destruction and shut out from the presence of the Lord and from the majesty of his power.
>
> Paul, in 2 Thessalonians 1:9

> Depart from me, you who are cursed, into the eternal fire prepared for the devil and his angels.
>
> Jesus, in Matthew 25:41

DiggiNG DeEpeR

✗ Lutzer, Erwin. *Your Eternal Reward: Triumph and Tears at the Judgment Seat of Christ.* Chicago: Moody Press, 1998.

✗ Wall, Joe. *Going for the Gold: Reward and Loss at the Judgment of Believers.* Chicago: Moody Press, 1991.

HELP FILE

YOU DON'T STILL BELIEVE IN HELL, DO YOU?

It might surprise you to know that Jesus talked more about hell than he did about heaven. Jesus was never afraid of or ashamed of the subject. He made it clear to people on several occasions that he believed in a place of judgment called *hell*.

Some people believe that God is too loving to send a person to hell. The God of the Bible, however, is not only loving but also holy and true. His love does not cancel out his holy hatred of sin and his promises to judge those who reject him.

Other people have concluded that human beings are too good to suffer in hell. They contend that God will certainly not allow his creatures to languish there eternally. They forget that God has declared that we are all corrupted by sin. We all fall far short of God's standard of perfection (Romans 3:23).

To be honest, I am very disturbed by the idea of hell. When I try to comprehend what hell will be like, my mind and heart struggle with every aspect of it. If the Bible did not make some clear declarations about the reality of hell, I would never be able to believe that hell exists.

But Jesus, who is the truth, taught more about hell than anyone else in the Bible. He didn't try to frighten people; he tried to warn them. And he offered himself in order to give us an alternative to hell.

A Real Place

The Bible describes two distinct places as hell. In Luke 16 Jesus talks about the torments of Hades (**hay**-deez), the place where the spirits of unbelieving persons go at death. Their bodies have been buried, but

GEHENNA

The Greek word *gehenna* (ge-**hen**-a) is used twelve times in the New Testament to refer to the place of eternal separation from God. It is translated as "hell" in the *New International Version*. *Gehenna* is the Greek transliteration of a Hebrew word that referred to a valley outside the southern city walls of Jerusalem. The valley was used as a garbage dump, and fires burned continually there. The word came to be used to describe the eternal separation and agony of hell. (Jesus uses the word *gehenna* in Matthew 5:22, 29 – 30; 10:28; 18:9; 23:15, 33; Mark 9:43, 45, 47; Luke 12:5.)

their spirits are consciously alive in Hades. The second place described in the Bible as hell is the final lake of fire.

Hades is a temporary place. The people who are today in Hades will be resurrected at the end of time to stand in judgment before God. They will not experience a resurrection to *life,* but a resurrection to *judgment* (John 5:28 – 29). Their bodies will be raised from the dead, but not in glory like the bodies of believers. Their bodies will survive forever, but in a place of separation from the conscious presence of God.

At the end of God's final judgment, every person who has rejected God's grace will be ushered into the final hell, the lake of fire. Death and Hades are thrown there too (Revelation 20:14). Six times in Matthew's Gospel, Jesus describes hell as "the fiery furnace," a place of "darkness," a place where there will be "weeping and gnashing of teeth" (Matthew 8:12; 13:42, 50; 22:13; 24:51; 25:30).

If you believe the theology of *The Far Side* cartoons, hell is Satan's place of power. He sits on a throne, ordering his little imps to do his bidding. The truth is that Satan fears

WHEN YOU'RE DEAD, YOU'RE DONE FOR

The average secularist, who gives little or no thought to God, believes that at death we simply cease to exist. The Bible, however, teaches that all human beings exist forever — either in conscious relationship with God or separation from God. As much as secularists and atheists may deny it, death is not the end of human existence.

Secularists aren't the only ones who think that some persons will cease to exist in the future. Some Christians believe that those who reject God's gift of salvation in Jesus will not be sent to an eternal place of conscious suffering. Instead, their eternal punishment will be annihilation; they will cease to exist.

Those who hold this view struggle with the idea that people will endure torment and pain forever. They may embrace the view

that unbelieving men and women will experience torment for a while, but eventually all unbelievers will suffer a second kind of death and will no longer exist. God's final judgment on the sinner, they believe, is annihilation.

Most Christians disagree with this view — not because we enjoy the thought of people suffering, but because the Bible seems so clearly to teach that hell is a place of eternal consciousness. The sufferings of unbelievers is said to last the same length of time as the blessings of those who believe, namely, *forever.* In Matthew 25:46 Jesus said that those who have no faith relationship with him will "go away to *eternal* punishment," while those who have followed him will enjoy "*eternal* life" (emphasis added). If the believer's conscious enjoyment of heaven is forever, so is the unbeliever's conscious experience of hell.

PURGATORY

The teachings of the Roman Catholic Church include belief in a place of purification called "purgatory." Catholic teaching says that those who die at peace with the church but who are not yet perfect must undergo purifying suffering. Purgatory prepares the soul for heaven by purging out sinful or unholy traits.

Belief in purgatory comes from the teaching authority of the Catholic Church and not directly from the Bible. Protestant Christians argue that no verse of Scripture supports a belief in purgatory. In the minds of most Protestants, purgatory devalues the full payment for sin that Jesus made on the cross. The apostle John says that "the blood of Jesus, [God's] Son, purifies us from *all* sin" (1 John 1:7, emphasis added). Jesus'

death and resurrection did for us what we could not do for ourselves. As Paul practically shouts in Romans 8:1: "There is now *no* condemnation for those who are in Christ Jesus" (emphasis added).

A related teaching of the Catholic Church is the possibility of a place called "limbo," where the spirits of infants reside in comfort for eternity. No passage of Scripture speaks directly to the issue of whether God redeems infants and those unable to believe (such as persons who have severe mental retardation). Most Christians believe that God saves them purely out of his grace and love. It is God's nature to rescue those who have no power to rescue themselves.

and hates hell. Hell is the place of his final judgment (Revelation 20:10). Satan is not the king of hell; God is.

The Good News about a Bad Place

The good news about hell is that hell is avoidable. It's optional; you don't have to go there. The Bible declares that *all* of us are lost. We are all sinners by nature and by choice. We deserve the hell the Bible describes. God would be perfectly just and fair if he condemned us all to an eternity separated from him. But in his grace God has provided a way of escape.

When we were enemies of God, plunging toward hell, God gave his Son, Jesus, to die on a cross in our place. On that cross Jesus took what we deserved. But the cross wasn't the end of the story. Three days later Jesus burst out of the grave — alive. He broke the power of sin and death and hell forever. Jesus offers salvation freely to all who will believe in him. He gives us life, eternal life — not death, not hell, not what we deserve, but what we *don't* deserve.

If you have believed in Jesus Christ as your Savior and Lord, you will never experience hell. Jesus took your hell on the cross. But if you reject Jesus and his gift of eternal life, you reject the only available sacrifice for sin. Without Jesus, you can plan on a certain future in a very real place called hell.

GOD'S FUTURE JUDGMENTS

Who	When	Where	Basis	Results
Believers in Jesus	At death or just after the rapture	Heaven	Faithfulness and obedience to Jesus	Reward or loss of reward
Believers from the Old Testament	Just after Jesus' return to earth	Earth	Faithfulness to the true God	Rewards
Tribulation believers	End of the Tribulation	Earth	Faithfulness under trial	Authority in the Kingdom
Antichrist and the false prophet	At Jesus' return to earth	Earth	Rebellion against God and his Son	Cast into lake of fire
Jews who survive the Tribulation	Just after Jesus' return to earth	Earth; in the desert	Faith in Jesus	Believers enter the Kingdom
Gentiles who survive the Tribulation	Just after Jesus' return to earth	Earth	Faith in Jesus demonstrated by deeds	Believers enter the Kingdom
Satan and evil angels	End of thousand-year reign of Jesus	Before God's great throne	Rebellion against God	Sent to the lake of fire
Unbelieving people from all ages	End of thousand-year reign of Jesus	Before God's great throne	Rejection of God's grace	Separated from God forever

CHAPTER 10

The Never-Ending Story: Heaven

The Never-Ending Story: Heaven

── Heads Up ──────────────

▸ Get ready for some good news! Heaven ahead!

▸ Heaven just keeps getting better

▸ What do you want to do with the rest of eternity?

If you've survived reading all the bad news about the future — the Tribulation, wars, judgment — you are ready for the good news! God has prepared a wonderful place for his people, a place called "heaven."

Unfortunately, some people don't get very excited when they think about heaven. They view it as an eternal church service — or they picture themselves sitting on a cloud, strumming a harp. There's no pain or tears, but for some reason it sounds so boring.

This popular picture of heaven is not the picture the Bible paints. Heaven is a place of activity, joy, and unlimited opportunity. No one will ever be bored!

In My Father's House: Heaven — Phase One

There are two paths a Christian may take to arrive in heaven. First path: We go to heaven when we die. In chapter 8 we explored what the Bible teaches about death. We learned that when a human being dies, the person's spirit is separated from the body. The body is dead. We bury the body or cremate the body, but the person no longer resides in that body. The spirit, or the soul, lives on.

The spirits of people who have received God's gift of salvation are taken "to heaven." We are immediately and consciously in the presence of Jesus Christ. The apostle Paul said that when we are "away from the body" in death, we are "at home with the Lord" (2 Corinthians 5:8).

Path two to get into heaven will be experienced by one generation of Christians only — the generation that will be taken to heaven in the rapture. When Jesus returns in the air for all his people (the rapture), the Christians who are alive on earth at that moment will be instantly changed and snatched away. We will not experience physical death. We will be taken directly into heaven.

The heaven we will enter at death or after the rapture is also called (by Jesus) "my Father's house." Jesus used this phrase in a conversation with his disciples just before he was crucified:

> Stop having a troubled heart. You already trust in God; now trust in me in the same way. In my Father's house are many dwelling places — I'm telling you the truth! And if I leave, I am leaving to prepare that place for you. Then I will come back and take you to be with me forever. (John 14:1 – 3, author's paraphrase)

Unfortunately, these verses have given people some inaccurate ideas about heaven! In the King James Version, a translation of the Bible

IS GRANDMA IN HEAVEN?

Jesus has been preparing the Father's house for nearly two thousand years, and it's already teeming with activity. Two groups inhabit heaven today.

First, heaven is the dwelling place of *God's angels*. Jesus often spoke of the angels "in heaven" (Matthew 18:10; Mark 12:25; 13:32). Angels care for those on earth who will inherit salvation (Hebrews 1:14), but they live in heaven.

The second group inhabiting heaven are the *spirits of believers who have died*. Those who have died after Jesus' resurrection will return with Jesus at the rapture, and their bodies will be resurrected. Those believers who died before Jesus' resurrection will wait for the beginning of Christ's Kingdom on earth to receive their new bodies, but they enjoy heaven today.

Angels and believing human beings join two others in heaven — *Jesus Christ* and *God the Father.* Forty days after his resurrection, Jesus ascended to heaven. Jesus returned to the glory he had with the Father before he came to earth as a human being.

We realize that heaven does not and cannot contain God the Father. He is pure spirit and is infinitely greater than his creation. But the Bible pictures heaven as the place where the Father displays his glorious presence. Moses, the great lawgiver, said, "Look down from heaven, your holy dwelling place, and bless your people" (Deuteronomy 26:15). When human beings are allowed to see into heaven, they perceive God as brilliant light or a burning ember.

used by English-speaking Christians for more than three hundred years, verse 2 reads: "In my Father's house are many *mansions*" (emphasis added) — which has led some Christians to believe that personal palaces await each of us. Songs and sermons and spirituals have been written about our glorious mansions in heaven. Don't get me wrong — heaven will surely be a place of incredible beauty and splendor, but please don't envision rows of mansions — a heavenly Beverly Hills, if you will! We will have a dwelling place (some scholars translate the Greek word *mone*m as "rooms," or "apartments"), but the focus of heaven will be on our fellowship with Jesus, not on the size of our house.

What we *can* learn from Jesus' words is that Jesus is preparing that *place* for us — and preparing *us* to dwell in that place. Two building projects are going on! As we respond obediently and faithfully to the trials and challenges we face in this life, we are being gradually changed to be like Jesus. Heaven is a prepared place for prepared people.

Jesus' promise to the disciples is that he will leave for a while, but will return some day to take them to be with him. But none of the disciples lived to see this promise fulfilled. All the disciples died. *Part* of Jesus' promise was fulfilled. They went to be with Jesus in the Father's house. They are there today, where they enjoy intimate friendship with Jesus. But the day will come when Jesus will return to take living Christians out of this world. Then Jesus will bring with him the spirits of the disciples and of all the followers of Jesus since then. They will get new bodies — we will get new bodies — and we will all return to the Father's house as resurrected human beings.

So "Heaven — Phase One" is a beautiful place of rest and joy. It's the place where Jesus is right now. But as wonderful as this place is, it's only temporary. An even better place is yet to come.

Heaven — Phase Two

At the end of the Tribulation, Jesus will return to earth in majesty, and we will come with him. Jesus destroys the Antichrist and his armies, and we have a grandstand seat for this final battle. Then Jesus sets up his Kingdom on earth, and we get to enjoy it. Yes, we are in eternal bodies and other people are in natural, earthly bodies, but we will coexist in the Kingdom.

FATHER ABRAHAM

Ever since Jesus rose from the dead we have had the assurance that Christians who die go to be with Jesus in heaven. But what about all those people who died *before* Jesus came to earth — all the people who trusted God and obeyed God, such as Abraham and Joseph and Ruth and David?

Jesus made it clear that the spirits of all who died before his resurrection went to a place called Hades — those who had rejected God went to a place of torment; those who had believed in the true God went to a place of comfort called "Abraham's side." (See Luke 16:19 – 24 for Jesus' words.)

When Jesus ascended into heaven forty days after his resurrection, he took all the believers' spirits with him to his Father's house. The only people in Hades today are unbelievers dwelling in the place of torment.

At the rapture, the spirits of Christians who have died after Jesus' resurrection will come back with Jesus to receive their resurrection bodies. Apparently Abraham and all his Old Testament buddies will wait to get their new bodies until Jesus returns to earth seven years later. The hope of believers in the Old Testament was to see Messiah's Kingdom on earth. They are resurrected at the beginning of that wonderful age of peace and enjoy its benefits for one thousand years. Jesus said that Christians and Old Testament believers would sit down together in the Kingdom of God and enjoy a great celebration feast together (Matthew 8:1). That's one buffet line you don't want to miss!

Don't get the idea that we will just sit around in the Kingdom. Far from it! The Bible doesn't spell out in detail everything we'll be doing, but it does talk about ruling over cities (Luke 19:17 – 19) and reigning with Jesus over a renewed earth (2 Timothy 2:12; Revelation 20:6).

So "phase two" of our experience of heaven will be a thousand years on the earth as God intended our earth to be. But even this experience is temporary. As the thousand-year Kingdom comes to an end, Satan is set free to organize one more rebellion. God quickly brings this rebellion to an end — and we will step back to see an even more magnificent work of God.

Heaven — Final Phase

After the resurrection of all believers to life and after the final judgment on all who have rejected God's grace, God will accomplish another transformation — not of our bodies, but of the universe!

This present universe is under a shroud. Adam's sin way back at the beginning affected everything in God's creation. The ground God had created to produce abundant food began to require human toil and sweat before it yielded a harvest (Genesis 3:17 – 19). Disease, deformity, and disaster all have their roots in the evil corruption of the world by sin. The apostle Paul saw the whole creation "groaning as in the pains of childbirth" (Romans 8:22).

Our earth and the universe around it are in the process of passing away, and some day they will come to an end. Sin's curse will be lifted during Jesus' Kingdom, but the corroding power of evil will have already made God's first creation unsuitable for our eternal home. The apostle Peter tells us exactly what will happen in the future:

> But by His word the present heavens and earth are being reserved for fire. . . .

> But the day of the Lord will come like a thief, in which the heavens will pass away with a roar and the elements will be destroyed with intense heat, and the earth and its works will be burned up. . . .

> The heavens will be destroyed by burning, and the elements will melt with intense heat! (2 Peter 3:7, 10, 12 NASB)

Peter is describing the total destruction of the earth and the planetary heavens around it. When Jesus has reclaimed the creation that was corrupted by sin, and when he has conquered every enemy, this present visible universe will evaporate with a thunderous roar. The energy held in the atomic structure of the elements will be released, and the old creation will vaporize. No special effects on that day! It will be the real thing.

When the old world is gone, God will step in and create a new place for his people. To his description of the world's destruction, Peter adds this: "We are looking forward to a new heaven and a new earth, the home of righteousness" (2 Peter 3:13).

New Things

In John's amazing vision of our future permanent home, he saw four new things. First, he saw a *newly created heaven* (Revelation 21:1). This is not just a patched-up, reworked edition of the old universe.

With his awesome power, God will fashion a new universe before our eyes.

Second, John saw *a new earth*, "for the first heaven and the first earth had passed away, and there was no longer any sea" (Revelation 21:1). Is this new earth going to be like our present earth? Probably not. I think it will be a world of beauty and order and wonder (like our present world), but there will also be some differences. No oceans will separate the nations or peoples of the new earth. Later on John sees an enormous city resting on the earth (Revelation 21:2) — a city that would throw our spinning earth out of orbit and into the sun! God's new earth probably won't rotate, because John says there is no night there (Revelation 21:15). If the new universe has a sun and moon, they won't be needed to light the earth, because the radiance of God lights it continuously (Revelation 21:23; 22:5).

Third, John saw that *everything in the future creation will be new*. "He who was seated on the throne said, 'I am making everything new!' " (Revelation 21:5). Heaven will be so unlike anything we are familiar with that our present language can't describe it. We will have to get new dictionaries in that new earth — filled with new words! Some things will be missing in the new creation, but they won't be missed. Sin's curse will be gone forever, along with the disease, decay, and injustice that came with it (Revelation 22:3). Death, mourning, suffering, and pain won't be there either. God will "wipe every tear from [our] eyes" (Revelation 21:4). There will be no tempter in heaven. Satan's worst nightmare will have come true. He will be confined to the lake of fire forever (Revelation 20:10). John saw no hospitals or cemeteries or prisons or entertainment that centered on immorality or exploitation. John didn't see any church buildings either. This fact will undoubtedly bother some people who are more committed to a

"Heaven will be the answer to every prayer, every desire for healing — physical, emotional, mental, and spiritual. All healings on earth are previews of coming attractions."

Quotation Marks

Peter Kreeft, in *Everything You Ever Wanted to Know About Heaven, but Never Dreamed of Asking* (Harrison, N.Y.: Ignatius, 1990), 79

denomination than to Jesus, but in this forever place the Lord God and Jesus the Lamb are the temple of worship.

The fourth "new" thing John saw in heaven was *a magnificent city:*

> I saw the Holy City, the new Jerusalem, coming down out of heaven from God, prepared as a bride beautifully dressed for her husband. And I heard a loud voice from the throne saying, "Now the dwelling of God is with men, and he will live with them. They will be his people, and God himself will be with them and be their God." (Revelation 21:2 – 3)

John describes our future, final home as a city with walls and gates and streets. The new Jerusalem will be a dazzling city, designed and built by God. It is a *holy* city too — uncorrupted by evil. This is the place where we will live forever.

The angel who gave John the guided tour of the new earth measured the city (Revelation 21:15). Its width, length, and height are equal, making a cube or pyramid fourteen hundred miles on each side. That's roughly the distance from the Mississippi River to the Atlantic Ocean and from the United States/Canadian border to the Gulf of Mexico. If that isn't massive enough, it stretches from earth's surface one-twentieth of the way to our moon — the size of a small planet! John doesn't say if the city rests on the new earth or if it's suspended above the new earth or if the city *is* the new earth. It's a challenge for John just to try to tell us what this magnificent eternal home of ours is like.

We will make millions of new friends in heaven. The city has twelve gates, not one (Revelation 21:12). People will enter the city from all directions. They will come from every ethnic group, from every level of society, from every direction on the theological compass, and from every generation since the beginning of time. But we will all be bound together by our faith in and devotion to the Lord Jesus Christ.

Forever Is a Long, Long Time

Our eternal home in the new city on the new earth sounds like a spectacular place — but if we are honest, we wonder if it won't get a little boring. One college student once asked me, "Is heaven just an endless church service?" She didn't sound too excited about going there.

Actually, heaven will be a place of complete fulfillment and limitless opportunities. I find five activities that will fill our lives in heaven.

Worship

We will spend time "in church," but it will be joyous, spontaneous, genuine worship. We will shout and sing praise to God — and we won't be distracted by time, we won't get tired physically, we won't be inhibited in our worship by what is accepted in our particular theological tradition. We will stand, kneel, and fall on our faces — and we won't care what those around us think. All we will care about is that God knows how much we love him. If you are expecting quiet, solemn worship in heaven, clothed in hushed tones and accompanied by soft organ music, you will be disappointed. Heaven's worship is punctuated by shouts, exuberant voices, trumpets, and spontaneous singing.

Ministry

The apostle John tells us eight times in the book of Revelation that part of our activity in heaven will be to serve God — "[God's] servants will serve him" (Revelation 22:3). We will serve without frustration, without fear of failure, without the exhaustion that so limits our ministries here on earth. The work will be enriching, challenging, and fulfilling beyond anything we've ever achieved in this life.

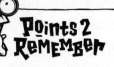

Points 2 Remember

- ☑ Christians who die (or are raptured) go to be with Jesus in the Father's house — but that is only "phase one" of heaven.

- ☑ Our eternal home will be a magnificent city on a new earth.

- ☑ Heaven will be a place of limitless opportunity, spontaneous worship, and joy-filled fellowship.

Fellowship

Heaven will give us time to enjoy the company of millions of believers — and Jesus himself (Hebrews 12:22 – 23). We will relax around the table with Elijah and Abraham and Paul and Mary — and we will have a lot to talk about. Instead of focusing on our own agendas, as we so often do here, we will be able to focus all our attention and energy on others.

Learning

We won't know everything when we get to heaven — but we will have an infinite capacity to learn. We will learn about each other, we will learn about God's newly created earth, we will learn more and more about our great God. The Bible says that in the coming ages God will take us deeper and deeper into the wonders of "the incomparable riches of his grace" (Ephesians 2:7). Think of all the things you've had an interest in doing but have never had the time or opportunity to pursue — playing the cello, rock climbing, learning to paint. Heaven will be a place of limitless opportunities.

Rest

Heaven will be a place of perfect wholeness. We will finally find rest. It won't be rest from work or weariness — resurrected bodies don't get tired! It will be rest from want, the empowering, energizing rest found in God's presence alone. In heaven we will be perfectly content and satisfied forever.

Sounds like a place you want to go to, doesn't it? But God hasn't told us about heaven's glory so that we'll dress in white robes and sit on a mountaintop waiting for Jesus to come. He's told us what lies ahead so that we'll live courageous, faithful lives here and now. Listen to what the apostle Peter focused on when he thought about heaven:

> Since everything will be destroyed in this way, what kind of people ought you to be? You ought to live holy and godly lives as you look forward to the day of God and speed its coming. . . .

> So then, dear friends, since you are looking forward to this, make every effort to be found spotless, blameless and at peace with him. (2 Peter 3:11 – 12, 14)

DigginG DeEpeR

X   Connelly, Douglas. *The Promise of Heaven*. Downers Grove, Ill.: InterVarsity Press, 2000.

This book explores what the Bible says about heaven and how our lives *now* make an impact on our lives *in the future*. (I've also written a Bible study guide titled *Heaven* in the LifeGuide series published by InterVarsity Press.)

HELP FILE

SEVEN HEAVY QUESTIONS ABOUT HEAVEN

1. Will We Recognize Each Other in Heaven?

I think we will! Jesus was recognized by his disciples after his resurrection. I think I will know my parents as my earthly parents and my children as my children. Even though Jesus made it clear that we will not reproduce in heaven (Matthew 22:30), I am confident I will know that Karen was my wife on earth. What we *won't* remember is who is missing in heaven. Those friends or family members who reject Jesus Christ and are condemned will be erased from our memories — along with the memories of our sins and failures and disobedience here on earth. Heaven would not be an experience without tears or pain if we had to live with regret over our past or with remorse for those separated from us.

2. When People (or Babies) Die, Do They Become Angels?

No! Human beings are human beings forever. We *never* become angelic beings. (Sorry if that throws a kink in your love for the TV show *Touched by an Angel*.) As glorious as angels are, resurrected human beings will have a majesty that surpasses even the angels. Don't ever wish to be an angel! God extended his love to us; Jesus died for us; heaven is a place prepared for us.

3. What Are Resurrection Bodies Like?

We will have an eternal body like Jesus' resurrection body (1 Corinthians 15:49; 1 John 3:2). These present bodies decay and die; our resurrection bodies will never die. (Read 1 Corinthians 15:42 – 44.) The only person in heaven who won't have a perfect body is Jesus. Even after his resurrection he still had the scars in his hands and feet from where he had been nailed to the cross. The wound in his side from the centurion's spear was still visible (John 20:27). Jesus will bear these redemptive scars forever as reminders of what he suffered for our salvation.

4. Will We See God in Heaven?

I do not think we will "see" God the Father. We will see what the apostle John and the prophet Ezekiel saw when they were allowed a glimpse into heaven — a figure of a person surrounded by brilliant light. The person we will see in heaven is Jesus, but we will see him as John saw him in Revelation 1 — an awesome, glorious Lord, exalted over all. We won't run up and shake hands with Jesus when we see him. John was Jesus' closest friend on earth, but when John saw the Lord sixty years after Jesus had gone to heaven, John didn't slap Jesus on the back and say, "It's so great to see you again." John fell on his face in adoration and worship (Revelation 1:12 – 17). We will only see Jesus in heaven, but he will be enough.

5. Are There Animals in Heaven?

The new heaven and the new earth created by God for our eternal home will be a place of incredible beauty and variety. I'm sure it will be even more fascinating than this world — and animals are a wonderful part of this world. So I am speculating that animals will grace the new world, too. Now, this doesn't mean your pet parakeet who died when you were in high school went to heaven! Animals don't have an eternal spirit. But I think one of the joys of heaven will be an abundant variety of animals.

6. Will We Experience the Passage of Time in Heaven?

Songs about heaven say there will be "no time there," but the Bible never says that. In fact, we have at least one hint that we *will* mark the passage of time. The apostle John saw the tree of life in heaven and was told that it bears "twelve crops of fruit, yielding its fruit *every month*" (Revelation 22:2, emphasis added). So we will experience the passage of time, but we will never age or grow old.

7. Do People in Heaven Today Know What's Happening on Earth?

We can't say with absolute certainty, but a couple of biblical statements imply that people in heaven do have some knowledge of events on earth. The writer of Hebrews encourages us to live faithful lives because we are surrounded by "a great cloud of witnesses" — and he has just talked about a whole bunch of people who were already in heaven (Hebrews 12:1; see the list of witnesses in Hebrews 11). Angels observe what we do (1 Corinthians 11:10), so why not believers in heaven? In Revelation 6:9 John looked into heaven and saw some "souls of those who had been slain." These were the spirits of people killed during the Tribulation for their loyalty to Jesus. These souls say to God, "How long, Sovereign Lord, holy and true, until you judge the inhabitants of the earth and avenge our blood?" (Revelation 6:10). These people knew that they had been killed unjustly (so they remembered some things — bad things — that had happened to them on earth), and they knew that God was in the process of judging the world (so they had at least a general idea of events on earth). They were then told that they would have to wait a little longer, because even more believers would have to die before God's judgment would be completed (so they knew more bad events were *about* to happen on earth). The indications are that people in heaven are aware of what is going on in the earthly realm. They have God's perspective on what's happening, as well as God's presence and power to comfort them, but they are aware at least of what God is doing on the earth.

CHAPTER 11

A Survival Guide for the Future

A Survival Guide for the Future

Heads Up

▸ Surviving the future involves preparation right now
▸ Find out how to practice your praise
▸ Keep looking for Jesus!

It happens every time! I had just spoken on the topic of biblical prophecy at a summer Bible conference when a well-dressed young woman came up, handed me her business card, and said something I'd heard many times: "I just don't like all this talk about the future. I'm much more concerned with the here and now. I've got a mortgage to pay, two kids to raise, a career to nurture, and I'm deeply involved at my church. What good is it to get all worked up over the future?"

My response was simple. I explained that what we know and believe about the future will profoundly affect what we do every day. It will affect how we do our jobs and how we raise our kids — and even how we pay off the mortgage!

The big question that emerges from our look at the Antichrist and the Kingdom and the various views of the rapture is this: What can we do today to get ready for God's tomorrow? Jesus said there would be two kinds of people on earth when he returned — the prepared and the unprepared.

One of Jesus' stories went like this: Ten women were waiting for the bridegroom to come. He was coming to claim his bride and to enter into the joyful celebration of the wedding feast. No one knew when the bridegroom would come. It might be within the hour, or it might be several hours away. All the women knew was that they didn't want to miss him. Each of the women had an oil lamp that they would hold high in the procession as it moved toward the wedding celebration. Five of the women brought extra oil; five only brought what the lamp held.

As time went by and the lamps ran out of oil, the five who were unprepared had to leave the waiting place to get more oil. While they were gone — you guessed it — the groom came by and swept the prepared women along with him into the celebration. The unprepared women were left outside. (You can read this parable for yourself in Matthew 25:1 – 13.)

So here's the question: If Jesus returns today, will you be prepared or unprepared? It doesn't make any difference what position you hold on when the rapture will occur or what view you take of how the Kingdom is to be perceived. Jesus said, "I will come again." If he comes today, will you be ready?

I can't answer this question for you — but I can give you some suggestions that will help keep eternity in the picture when you face the demands of another day. If you work through these tactics with a sincere heart, you will be rapture-ready!

Survival Tactic #1: Solidify Your Relationship with the Coming King

When Jesus comes, it will be too late! When you die, there is no second chance. The most critical decision you can make about the future is to believe in Jesus Christ.

The Bible says that we are all lost, separated from God by our sin (Romans 3:23). That's not my judgment on you; that's what *God* says — and I'm included too. That's the bad news. None of us deserve heaven. The good news is that God has found a way to satisfy his justice against our willful disobedience and at the same time to rescue us from the dreadful consequences of sin.

God himself was willing to pay the penalty we deserved to pay. Jesus — God the Son — came to earth and died on a cross, bearing in his body and in his spirit the judgment we deserved. Jesus' death on the cross was the full payment for our sins. Jesus' resurrection from the dead was the proof that our sins are forgiven and removed. Now Jesus offers salvation, cleansing, a new heart, a new life to all who will receive his gift. It's a gift given freely to all who will believe.

Jesus' promise is that those who believe in him and follow him receive eternal life — a whole new kind of life. When Jesus returns, he will look for those who are linked to him in a relationship of faith.

If you have never believed in Jesus, you aren't ready for the future. You may think that you will be accepted by God in some other way. You may try to get into heaven through good deeds or by going to church, but Jesus said, "*I* am the way" (John 14:6, emphasis added). We come into a right relationship with God in only one way — by believing in Jesus and receiving his gift of life.

Survival Tactic #2: Live as a Committed Follower of Jesus

We are saved by God's grace alone — but once we come to faith, God calls us to a life of joyful obedience to him. God not only calls us, he also equips us. He gives us natural abilities, spiritual gifts, resources of time and money, and wonderful opportunities to serve him. God gives abundantly, and he expects us to invest into his Kingdom what he gives us. Most of us give very little thought to our future evaluation before the Lord, but that day is coming — and we will all be there.

Jesus told several instructive stories about a wealthy man who was leaving on a long journey. In each case the man entrusted his servants with his money while he was gone. In the parable recorded in Matthew 25:14 – 30, the master divides up his money among three servants. Each servant is given a share of the master's money according to his ability.

The first servant receives five talents of money. (A talent was a large weight; one talent of gold represented about twenty years' salary for the average worker. Do the math and you'll get some idea of the funds each man had at his disposal.) When the master returns, the first servant gives his account. He had invested the master's money wisely and worked hard at managing the funds, so that his return was an additional five talents.

"Well done," the master says. "You are a man I can trust. You've been faithful with a few things; I will put you in charge of many things." The first servant has a great performance review and gets a promotion and a bonus — just the words we like to hear from our boss!

The second servant receives two talents of money. He is not as experienced as the first servant, but he sees this as an opportunity to demonstrate his resourcefulness. When the master returns, the second servant has gained two additional talents. He hears the same commendation from the master — "Well done, good and faithful servant."

I wish I knew *how* these servants doubled their master's money. Imagine the book sales and seminar schedules these guys could pull down if they could teach us how to double our money over a few months' time. What surprises me is that the master didn't even ask how they did it! He just praises them for their accomplishments.

The third servant in the story takes a different approach. He takes the master's one talent of money (still some big bucks!) and buries it. He even had his speech to the master all worked out: "You are a hard man to please, sir. I was so afraid of losing your money that I hid it in the ground — but it's all right here. I haven't lost a cent!"

You want to feel sorry for this guy — but please don't. The master says that he is wicked and lazy. The servant wasn't afraid. He wanted to swing the golf clubs all day or lie around in a hammock, sipping iced tea. He didn't even walk to the bank to deposit the money so he could gain a little interest. He just dug a hole, dropped in the money, and took a nap to restore his sapped strength.

The master takes away even what the servant has and then has the servant banished from the party that is held to celebrate the master's return. The lazy servant stands outside, consumed with regret and shame.

We don't have much trouble understanding what Jesus says. The painful part is *applying* what he says to our lives. I think the hardest truth to face in this parable is the fact that God has entrusted us with different levels of giftedness. We all receive spiritual resources, but some of us are five-talent servants, some are two-talent servants, and some are one-talent servants. God doesn't do it to make us jealous. The gifts are the Master's to give as he desires. What he looks for is *faithfulness* in using these resources. The master in the story doesn't even tell the servants how to do it or what level of return he expects from them. He just lets them use his resources where they can be most effective.

Most Christians, I'm afraid, are like the third servant. We have no strategy for using our resources for the Lord. We can't even tell someone what our gifts are. We don't look with eager expectation for ways to invest God's resources. We wait until we are begged to take on some ministry responsibility — and then our main concern seems to be when our stint will be over.

Jesus will immediately see through all our excuses and fabrications. When opportunities arise to minister in some way to the body of Christ, some of us are experts at coming up with excuses for getting out of it. I wonder how these excuses will sound in Jesus' ears.

Jesus' point in telling the story (and my point in repeating it) is to show that our faithfulness to Jesus today affects our future. In the future Kingdom of God on earth, Christians will reign with Jesus. We will be responsible to oversee the Kingdom in some way. Those who have been faithful and intentional about investing their gifts and resources in God's work in this age will have greater responsibility given to them in that future age. Dedicated, sacrificial service is rewarded by greater opportunity to serve the Master. The faithful servants in the parable were not sent into retirement but given even more challenging tasks to perform.

So our view of the future has a direct impact on how you and I do our work today. We aren't just punching the clock to pay the rent. We are working to please our *real* boss, Jesus Christ (Colossians 3:23 – 24). How faithful we are in the small things now — paying the mortgage, raising our kids, serving on the church worship team, and so forth — will affect our level of responsibility in the future. If you want the future to be as challenging and fulfilling as it can be, faithfully serve God now in every arena of life.

1 Corinthians 4:5

Therefore judge nothing before the appointed time; wait till the Lord comes. He will bring to light what is hidden in darkness and will expose the motives of men's hearts. At that time each will receive his praise from God.

People around you may not notice or appreciate your dedicated obedience to Jesus, but the day will come when all the hard work of commitment will return to you multiple times. People may forget, but Jesus does not.

Survival Tactic #3: Practice Your Praise!

When Jesus wanted to picture what our "forever home" would be like, he didn't picture it as a church service or a theological lecture or even a quiet but boring retirement home. Jesus pictured heaven as a party — a joy-filled, foot-stomping, hug-your-Aunt-Mildred family reunion! We will sit down with Abraham and all the other well-known and lesser-known children of God for a wonderful, warm experience we only catch snatches of here on earth.

At the center of everything will be Jesus. Our songs, our praise, our adoration will be focused on him. We won't feel rushed. We won't get tired. Best of all, we will be totally unthreatened and uninhibited. We won't care what other people think of us; we will only care that Jesus knows how much we love him.

Because heaven is going to be such a celebration, maybe we should work at bringing a little more spontaneous joy into our lives and into our gatherings with other Christians right now. You might start a real revolution at your church or in your Bible study group or simply when you get together with Christian friends if you smile — or laugh — and shout in praise to God. Get some practice being happy as a Christian! It will prepare your heart for a joy-filled eternity.

"If you're not allowed to laugh in heaven, I don't want to go there."

Martin Luther

Quotation Marks

Survival Tactic #4: Keep Learning

Don't stop studying Bible prophecy just because you've come to the end of this book. Check out some of the other resources I've given you. Visit the prophecy section in your local Christian bookstore. Keep reading the Bible with an interest in the predictions that have yet to be fulfilled.

But now you can look at prophecy books or scan Web sites with a solid foundation of knowledge. You aren't going to be swayed by sensational new insights into the identity of the Antichrist or new calculations for the date of Jesus' return. Refuse to be a date setter or a date suggester — and refuse to buy into someone's ministry who follows that path. Just do what the Bible says: Live each day as though Jesus could return at any moment.

The only other suggestion I would make is that you read more widely than you may have before. Don't just listen to the speakers and read the books that support the position you hold. Listen to what other Christians are saying, and measure everything (including your own position) against the Word of God.

Survival Tactic #5: Keep Looking for Jesus

We don't look for "signs" that the Tribulation is approaching — although we certainly need to be aware of the events in the world around us. We don't look for the Antichrist — although he may be on the world scene right now. *We look for Jesus to return.* Paying the mortgage, raising the kids, and pursuing a career are all important aspects of life — but they are not all there is to life. Overshadowing our steps, encouraging our hearts, keeping us faithful when it would be easier to bail out is the rock-solid assurance we have that **Jesus is coming.**

The apostle John concludes the book of Revelation with a short burst of prayer — "Amen. Come, Lord Jesus" (Revelation 22:20). These are the very words that spring to our minds and lips as we look ahead: "We're ready, Lord. Come!"

Christians are sometimes accused of being so heavenly minded that we aren't much earthly good. I really don't think that's the problem. The Bible challenges us to set our hearts and minds on things above, not on

Points 2 Remember

☑ Jesus said there would be two kinds of people on earth when he returns — prepared and unprepared.

☑ The most crucial decision you can make about the future is to believe in Jesus.

☑ Our faithfulness to Jesus here and now affects our responsibilities and opportunities in the future.

☑ Get ready for a joy-filled forever!

earthly things (Colossians 3:1 – 2). God has not told us about the future so that we will live irresponsible and lazy lives. He has told us about the future so that we will live courageous and holy lives every day. We know how God's story ends, and we have nothing to fear from the world around us. Confidence in God and in his promises gives us the courage we need to walk through the fire of persecution — or to walk into the familiar workplace tomorrow morning.

The apostle Peter still says it best:

> Since everything will be destroyed in this way, what kind of people ought you to be? You ought to live holy and godly lives as you look forward to the day of God and speed its coming. . . .

> So then, dear friends, since you are looking forward to this, make every effort to be found spotless, blameless and at peace with him. (2 Peter 3:11 – 12, 14)

A Word of Thanks

No good book is produced without the wisdom and encouragement of others. I have been blessed beyond measure by the people who helped me with this one. An adult Sunday school class at Davison Missionary Church listened to most of this material, and their enthusiasm made the writing fun. Jim Keller, Alan Yerke, Allen Sudmann, Mike Ross, and Steve Aikman held me up in prayer and in friendship. Jack Kuhatschek, Dirk Buursma, and the team at Zondervan were exceptionally supportive in making this book available to a wider audience.

No one, however, has surpassed my wife, Karen, in her encouragement, love, and consistent belief that God was using my writing ministry to touch the lives of more people than I could imagine. She and my parents, Paul and Mary Connelly; my children, Kim, Kyle, Kevin, and Julie; and my sweetie, Allison (my granddaughter), make every day a joy.